© 2012 by

ISBN 978-

First Pub

This edition published 2013 by HLS Publishing Solutions

sue@inspiration-coaching.com

DEDICATION

I dedicate this book to the people who want to use their power of influence to empower other people to be the best they can be!

I hope that the ideas in this book serve you in creating a special coaching environment where everyone discovers their greatness and magnificence and can go on to inspire others to do so.

Sue Rutson

THANK YOU

To my family, especially Anneliese, Paul James and Kristen who have put up with losing me for hours to the computer!

Those who have helped to edit

Bev Woodcock

Ian Brendish

Vanessa Hollis

Those who have influenced:

Bruce Farrow of Helford 2000

To coaches who have inspired me personally

Ron Methven

Ray Learney

Haj Bhania

CONTENTS

FOREWORD

I have been in the business of exploring the development of human potential, and the psychology of motivation and behaviour for over 30 years.

I have been a sports fan for much longer! So combining those two interests when gaining my degree in Psychology in 2000 was an exciting - and enlightening - experience for me.

I now have a hunger for more knowledge in these areas. As a result I read avidly on the subject - it is one of my passions.

This book clearly shows the passion of the author for her sport, and the players. In sport as in life, passion brings out the best in all involved. Combining knowledge, experience, and the ability to bring out the best in coaches, tutors and players is a very special skill. Sue has this skill in bucket loads! She also has the rare ability to communicate this skill, and has done so in this book.

Anyone interested in improving their knowledge and understanding of the mental side of sport - and life, and how to apply them, will definitely benefit from reading this book.

Sue's passion for empowering others will keep you reading, eager to know more!

Ian Brendish

PRAISE FOR
SUE RUTSON

From individual delegates:

"Fantastic! Really enjoyable day, I learnt a lot about myself in terms of how I communicate with others. The exercises were interesting and enlightening and out of my comfort zone (good), would like more!"

"I have learnt to get on with life and forget about bad past memories and how to keep my head straight when feeling in different moods. I found it very interesting and helpful."

"I found Sue's very informative 3 week course far too short! It was fun, insightful and has changed my life forever!   Thank you Sue"

"I enjoyed the course very much. It was helpful and useful in my work life and home/social life. I would want to know more especially how to train my voice on public / personal speaking. It gave me a taster and would be interested to read more about the subject."

"I found Sue's attitude / teaching skills very good. It made you think and wish to learn more – three weeks was not really long enough. However I really learnt a lot and hope to put it into practice.   Thank you Sue"

"Very helpful learning experience. Sue's skills very well put. Teaching excellent. I enjoyed the three weeks very much."

PREFACE

"Our key to greatness lies not in our ability to project ourselves to others. Rather, our key to greatness lies in who we are which we can give to other people in a way that when they walk away from us, they are able to say in their hearts that they have taken away something with them quite extraordinary."

C. JoyBell C.

If you are not passionate about being an extraordinary coach, I advise you to put this book down now! This book doesn't focus on SPORT; rather, it focuses on PEOPLE. Have you noticed how some people can make a massive impact in a matter of seconds? They light up the room and manage to get anyone to do anything for them. What do these people have, and how can we achieve the same results?

When someone walks into a coaching session, coaches only get to see a tiny percentage of that person, and how they think, behave, learn, and what values and beliefs they have. By getting to know and understand the hidden areas of your athletes, and understanding how you directly influence them, you are using the 'Coaching Edge'.

This book is an introduction to mastering coaching people as individuals on the deeper, hidden level. In order to do this, you will need to apply certain skills to yourself, and by carrying out the exercises in this book you will soon notice some great results.

This work is based on a life-time of working with children and adults within sport and life, my own coaching experiences, tutoring and assessment of coaches, working as a personal development trainer and coach and NLP practitioner, my own continual development and learning, and is a work of passion.

The content incorporates a positive coaching style, with chapters and activities to help coaches develop skills, and provides tools to deliver positive coaching effectively. Using a positive coaching style isn't necessarily easy, but it is certainly a simple concept that has incredible results for you the coach, and more importantly, for your athletes.

"If you want to work with people then you need to work on yourself first!"

Sue Rutson

INTRODUCTION

"Coaches who can outline plays on a blackboard are a dime a dozen. The ones who win, get inside their players and motivate."

Vince Lombardi

Coaching as a profession is becoming increasingly popular. It is now so easy to qualify that the market is becoming flooded, and almost every weekend there are brand new coaches joining the workforce. This is an excellent situation for sport and for athletes looking for that 'right coach', because there is plenty of choice for them. But what about the coaches? How do they become established; how do they make their mark and attract athletes to their own sessions?

With so many coaches now in the market, why is it at meetings I hear organisers complaining that they can't find the 'right' coach? They express unhappiness that the coaches are drilling their groups, and pushing them to become good at the sport even when most of the children or adults merely want a 'fun' session! Sports organisers are looking for coaches with qualities that draw people into the sport, that have a certain charisma and who motivate, inspire and who KNOW how to meet the needs of the group!

Having studied, trained and assessed coaches, and coached professionally myself for over 23 years, I have put together my thoughts on what makes a great coach to share with others. All the ideas have been applied and have had successful results. Some coaches will find the ideas interesting, and may put them into practice themselves. Others could possibly find their belief system about coaching threatened, but nevertheless, when you have had a go at some of these ideas, you will discover the empowering changes that will be created both for yourself and for your athletes.

Within these pages we will be looking at:

- Adopting a positive coaching style

- A coach's personal presentation based on their appearance, body language, attitudes, and personality attributes and how this affects the athlete

- Communication skills of the coach. This includes advanced communication skills based on NLP techniques

- Techniques to affect the unconscious thinking of the athlete to help create change

- Visualisation, anchoring and other NLP techniques

- Activities to practice and develop the skills that are introduced.

Positive coaching is vastly different from the usual coaching idea of focussing on what is weak or wrong with the athlete and concentrating on putting this right! Whilst it is certainly important to improve weak areas, positive coaching focuses directly on finding out exactly what the athletes are doing right, and reinforcing the strengths of each athlete. It is a method that supports the athlete to do more things right and creates self-confidence and self-worth; it induces a wonderful working environment where the athlete feels valued, and, as a result, is receptive to being corrected. Finally and importantly, positive coaching meets the athletes' emotional needs.

A positive coach focuses on the athletes' mastery of their skills as opposed to the score; they see victory through the quest of excellence. They focus on effort instead of outcome, and learning instead of comparison to others.

A positive coach sets high standards of continuous improvement for himself and his athletes. He provides encouragement to every athlete, regardless of their standard, and encourages them to be, and to do, the best they can, both as athletes and as people.

A positive coach understands that mistakes are an essential part of learning and encourages his athletes to accept their mistakes as a learning opportunity, and to look for the learning each time.

A positive coach understands the importance of meeting his athletes' emotional needs and knows how to do this with specific advice and honest praise. He gives critical feedback in a positive manner that never undermines the athletes' self-worth.

A positive coach manages discipline and order in positive ways. Every athlete within a group is listened to, and is involved in decisions that affect their training. The positive coach remains upbeat and optimistic even when things are going wrong and encourages his athletes to do likewise. He recognises that when things go wrong the conduct of the coach is extremely important and can have a lasting effect. And when things do go wrong, the coach behaves impeccably to opponents, to umpires, and everyone involved. He understands the lessons that are being taught to his athletes and treats EVERYONE with absolute respect at all times. Above all a positive coach demonstrates and teaches integrity and would rather lose than to win with dishonour.

"Sports do not build character. They reveal it."

John Woode

1

POSITIVE

COACHING

"The world's a stage and most of us are desperately unrehearsed."

Sean O'Casey

Positive coaching begins with the coach, with their own attitude, delivery, focus, language patterns, voice, body language, beliefs, and values.

It is your decision alone that decides what the most important criteria for being a great coach is, and every coach develops their own style of coaching. Your individual personality and skill set has a direct impact on the delivery, and athletes will sort out which coach they prefer to meet their own preferences.

If you like to put your athlete first and are keen to adopt a positive coaching style where better to start than with yourself?

Why should we put some focus on ourselves and our own development? We may take our responsibilities as a role model for granted and know we have plenty of background knowledge; we become experienced at working with groups and individuals and develop a vast number of practice ideas. We are taught all these things in most coaching programmes and we are given feedback on how we use all these skills whilst we train.

So the question remains, why are some coaches more successful than others? Why does a coach who has less technical knowledge than another, have bigger classes, or achieve more successful results? What is the secret formula that gets a group motivated?

Let's take a trip down memory lane just for a moment, think back to school, clubs, sports etc.

How many teachers, leaders, coaches etc. can you remember? There must have been plenty over at least 10 plus years of education! Can you remember their names, or what they looked like? Why do you remember these particular ones? Is it because they created some sort of positive or negative emotion in you which made you feel good or bad about yourself? If so, then what did they do to create these emotions and what implication does this have on you now, as a coach? Do you think you are already remembered by many of your athletes, and if so what for? There are many teachers and coaches who are soon forgotten. This could be for many reasons but I wouldn't be surprised if it is because they lacked personality, energy, presentation skills, or they weren't excited about the work they were doing!

Do you want to be remembered, and if so what for?

I want to be remembered for

....

In order to adopt a positive coaching style it is important to put the athlete first. This means that whatever is happening in our own life, however bad it may be needs to be left at the door. Would we tune into a radio station if we had to listen to the D.J's moaning, talking in monotonous tones, or being snappy and angry with those they are presenting with? I don't think so! But coaches are people too, with our own problems and issues that affect how we feel!

In order to prepare for positive coaching we need to step up to dealing with our problems, or at the very least, use good coping mechanisms so that our 'moods' or negative emotions have no adverse effect on the group. One of the most powerful life skills you can possess is the ability to control your response to people and events around you.

Having such personal control is an essential component of human excellence and achievement. Your ability to positively manage your reactions affects your behaviour, and in turn, directly affects your results.

Perception is projection. What we see in others is the shadow of ourselves that we don't admit to! How do you like that? This simply means that on two levels the coach is responsible for their relationships with athletes. For instance a coach's emotional state has an effect on how the coach interacts with their groups. Similarly the beliefs of a coach will greatly influence what they project.

Long ago in a small, far away village, there was place known as the House of 1000 Mirrors. A small, happy little dog learned of this place and decided to visit. When he arrived, he bounced happily up the stairs to the doorway of the house. He looked through the doorway with his ears lifted high and his tail wagging as fast as it could. To his great surprise, he found himself staring at 1000 other happy little dogs with their tails wagging just as fast as his. He smiled a great smile, and was answered with 1000 great smiles just as warm and friendly. As he left the

House, he thought to himself, "This is a wonderful place. I will come back and visit it often."

In this same village, another little dog, who was not quite as happy as the first one, decided to visit the house. He slowly climbed the stairs and hung his head low as he looked into the door. When he saw the 1000 unfriendly looking dogs staring back at him, he growled at them and was horrified to see 1000 little dogs growling back at him. As he left, he thought to himself, "That is a horrible place, and I will never go back there again."

YES, perception is projection indeed. I am no longer surprised that when I am feeling a bit jaded or a bit tired and below par, this is the session that is hardest to deliver. This is when I find challenging behaviours harder to manage and then I remember, "Life rocks if you rock", "Life is not how you find it, it's how you make it!"

Wow, being responsible is such a responsibility!

I remember a candidate coach who said that ALL children are difficult and don't listen. What a belief this candidate had! In fact, when I saw his coaching delivery, I wasn't at all surprised at how he came to his belief! I wonder whatever became of him. I think this is a good example of perception is projection, of getting the expectation you created.

As the leader of the group, as the coach, you set the tone. Your body language and your voice show and create energy levels, joy, humour, sadness, depression, anger etc. Every emotion is shown and is picked up by those around you, especially children and they react to what they 'find'. These emotions or traits are picked up by the subconscious and the group soon reflect back to you what you are projecting to them! So does this mean that you are responsible for inattention, low group energy or hyper-energy? Well, I would suggest that mostly yes you are! This is why it is important for the coach to take time on the journey to the coaching session to leave behind any negative emotions/feelings, and to create within themselves an inner feeling which is positive and appropriate to the session about to be led.

Some simple methods to get over the unwanted emotions and to prepare yourself to deliver in a 'positive' state are:

Relaxation – listening to your own preferred music.

Laughter – watch or listen to something that simply makes you laugh!

Create a state – simply think of a time, a specific time, when you felt in a great emotional state where, you were happy, or relaxed, or confident, or strong, or felt in control, anything that would be appropriate for you to feel before a coaching session. As you go back to that time now.......go right back, float down into your body and see what you saw, hear what you heard and really feel those feelings of being totally happy, or relaxed, confident etc. Do this several times and notice the changes.

Erase your stress - Imagine yourself in a theatre, alone, projecting a movie with your stress or your miserable situation on the screen. Then visualize a very big eraser in your hand and see yourself erasing the picture of your stress. Start in one corner of the screen and keep erasing slowly, bit by bit, all the pictures on the screen, until the screen is empty. Now project a new movie onto the screen in which you see yourself managing the situation positively and having the success you long for.

Breathe deeply at a relaxed pace - Do you hold your breath when you are stressed? When you hold your breath, your body does not get enough oxygen, which causes even more stress! When you notice you are holding your breath, take this as a signal to give yourself permission to breathe deeply at a relaxed pace.

Put Down Your Bags - Simply and metaphorically put everything that could be worrying you or the things you need to remember to do, anything at all that is not helpful to the coaching session, into a big sack and leave this in the car or at the door, or with your kit. You know you still have them, and can pick everything back up again once your session is finished, and the process will clear your head from any unhelpful clutter so that you are free to concentrate and enjoy the coaching experience fully.

Write a Letter - Write a letter to a person you are mad at, or to somebody that disappointed you. Write down everything you ever wanted to say to that person. Don't withhold anything. Go on writing until you feel calm again and you feel you have poured everything out. Burn this letter or cut it into pieces and throw it away. This technique will help you to get rid of YOUR emotions and may well change your perception of this person. This will also make the person much more open towards you, as they will feel that your energy has become less hostile.

All these methods are effective ways to create a positive state and can be learnt easily; everyone is able to choose which method suits them best. All coaches know that practicing will soon create new behaviours. We are very aware in our profession that good practice repeated often enough has a dramatic effect.

Take a moment to think about how you 'feel' when you are going to lead your coaching session, and whether there are any changes you can make to help you be more energised or inspiring when coaching.

What changes are you going to make?

....

....

....

....

....

....

....

....

"It all has to do with the director, the captain of the ship. He sets the pace, the mood. If the director is quiet, the set is quiet. If the director is loud, then everybody has to be louder to be heard."

Eva Marie Saint

"The thing with pretending you're in a good mood is that sometimes you can begin to believe it's true."

Charles de Lint

2

PERSONAL

PRESENTATION

"A good stance and posture reflect a proper state of mind."

Morihei Ueshiba

When wandering around the shops or anywhere there are lots of people, have you ever spent time looking at them, and been conscious that you can easily make assumptions about many of them? The way they dress often leads to assumptions of how they may feel about themselves, however, even more important is the message we pick up from their posture! Someone who stands erect gives off an aura of pride and self-confidence, and authority, while a person who slumps and stoops, gives an aura of lack of self-confidence and lacks authority.

Look around a crowded dining area or cafeteria some time, and notice how many people are hunched over their meals. Then try to spot someone who's sitting tall in their seat, raising their fork or spoon to their mouth instead of pitching forward to grab the next bite. Doesn't that look more elegant? Which person looks poised and confident to you?

But what is good posture anyway, and why is it so important? Basically, posture refers to the body's alignment and positioning with respect to the ever-present force of gravity. Whether we are standing, sitting or lying down gravity exerts a force on our joints, ligaments and muscles. Good posture entails distributing the force of gravity through our body so no one part of the structure is overstressed.

Your parents were right – Posture is Important!

The benefits to coaches having good posture are:

Portrays a confident image - A coach who projects a confident image will gain the trust and confidence of their athletes quickly and easily.

Breathing becomes easier and deeper - Diaphragmatic breathing which results in the inflation of the lower lobes of the lungs, activates the parasympathetic nervous system, which calms your mind and body. Having enough oxygen means that we have higher energy levels and are more alert.

Your voice will sound better - Being an effective communicator is an important element for a coach. Good posture means we are able to breathe more effectively which means that we can improve our voice quality and project out effectively. This is essential when coaching large groups.

Affects your frame of mind - Posture affects your frame of mind and, conversely, your frame of mind can affect your posture. So, when you are well, feeling happy and on top of things, posture tends to be upright and open. In contrast, people who are depressed and in chronic pain, often sit or stand slumped.

Healthy spine - Correct posture is a simple but very important way to keep the many intricate structures in the spine healthy. If coaches are standing for long periods of time then having a healthy spine is essential to staying active and working!

So, what are you waiting for? Start improving your posture right now!

How to Create Good Posture: Stand and walk with your head up, chin level with floor, shoulders relaxed and keep your lower abdomen flat. Imagine you have a piece of string attached to the top of your head holding you up and running down the centre of your body, pulling you upwards. This imaginary string is your centre line and your body weight should be balanced through this line, and supported by the weight bearing arches of your feet.

Standing still with relaxed knees, and good posture allows the coach to generate a rock solid image, which generates credibility and authority, and in turn helps the coach to master good delivery.

*Scientific test results show that not only does our posture effect what other people think about us; it actually has a direct affect on how we actually think about ourselves!*Finds." Science Daily 5 October 2009. 3 July 2010*

Centring - being in balance: Why is being centred and in balance important? Have you ever noticed a presenter/leader/coach talking to the group and shifting from foot to foot, or swaying to and fro? You may consider that the group views them as uncertain; he could lose the full attention of his audience. Indeed could this be where the term 'He's a push-over' comes from? Being centred and standing in balance builds authority and credibility, which is good news for coaches.

A good coach, just like any other leader or good communicator, should have about them some sort of 'presence'. That special intangible something that people are unconsciously aware of, that makes them 'sit up and take notice'. People who are natural leaders don't have to learn this because it is something they emanate without effort. For others though, there are some simple ideas described in this book, which when applied, can make a massive positive effect on the presentation and communication skills of any coach.

The activity below demonstrates the difference in body strength using a very simple to learn exercise. This affects the whole person, and helps you to look confident and grow in personal power.

****

Activity:

Finding your 'Centre'

Ask a friend to help with this and ask permission to touch them.

Ask your friend to simply stand next to you.

Put your hand on one of their shoulders and gently push them backwards.

What do you notice?

Let your friend do the same to you, and what do you notice again?

Now tell your friend to stand with their feet hip width apart, feet pointing straight ahead. Get them to imagine a string pulling them up from the top centre of the head. Tell them to place their index finger on their belly-button and notice a point just where their third finger is, (about 2.5 inches below their belly button. Now they are to bring ALL their thoughts, all their thinking down to that point whilst keeping their posture, and when they are ready, to let you know. This may take a few seconds, so make certain they have followed your instructions.

Now place your hand once again onto their shoulder and again gently push them backwards.

What do you notice this time?

Allow your friend to do the same to you, and what do you notice?

Bring your thoughts/thinking, back up to your head and do the above exercise again

What do you notice?

If you have followed the instructions you will notice the 'solidness' of the body when the thinking is brought down to your 'centre'. This creates an inner strength and has a dramatic positive, strengthening effect on communication skills.

****

The mind affects our physiology and our physiology also affects our mind so what is your posture/physiology like right now?

ACTION: Have a go at applying the suggestions in this chapter and then go back and re-read it with your athletes in mind! What learning can be applied to athletes? How do they present themselves to their opposition when they walk on the pitch or sporting arena? Are they centred and confident? How can you encourage, or teach your own athletes to create a good posture as they arrive to compete, and what difference could this make to their results?

"I have never known a really chic woman whose appearance was not in large part, an outward reflection of her inner self".

Mainboch

3

SELLING YOUR SESSION

"Everyone lives by selling something."

Robert Louis Stevenson

What is it about you and your coaching session that attracts players along? Do you gain athletes so well that your sessions are full and you have a waiting list? What is your athlete retention level like? Do you gain some and lose them quickly, or keep them for years? How do you stand out from the average coach?

To be a great coach, it isn't enough to just know a sport and its intricacies well. Neither is it merely being able to design practices and organise groups, communicate well, motivate, inspire, lead, be a role model.........it is all these things and more.

One factor that is often neglected in coach training is the presentation of the coaching session. This includes all the above elements, mixed with a personal delivery style and, last of all, sales techniques! Yes, we have to 'sell' ourselves and our session, and, even more importantly, we must sell the learning to our group, at every session, before we begin to deliver it!

Think about the following to help sell yourself and your session.

The coach

Dress appropriately for the group/session you are coaching; what are the groups' expectations of you the coach? If you consider yourself a professional coach with a serious group of athletes, then dress accordingly. If you expect high standards from your athletes in terms of sports specific clothing and trainers, then ensure you show this in your own dress. If you expect your athletes to remain safe because their trainers are suitable, clean, and have tied laces, your own footwear should reflect this. Remember at all times, what you see in your athletes is what you project!

Moods and energy are reflected back at you from your group! Expecting excellence and success usually means that you will get that back from your group. If you smile, love coaching and enjoy being with young people then your group will enjoy their session with you!

The most important consideration should be investing constantly in your own personal development. Developing your own skills, particularly in the areas of communicating and understanding people, is a way to achieve excellence and to get the best results from your own athletes.

Get to know your athletes

When parents bring their children along to their first session, greet parent/s and children warmly, and then speak to the child! It is important to build rapport with the parent because they are paying you. It is even more important to get to know the child because he or she is who you are going to be working with! What do they like to do, what motivates them, what makes them laugh, who are their friends? Making conversation with each athlete on a 'personal' and professional level means that you will know how to motivate and inspire them, and it builds trust, allowing them to feel acknowledged and significant, and therefore empowers them to build confidence and self-esteem. Even more importantly, it encourages them to have a voice, and to share their own thoughts on their performance.

Code of conduct

Give special thought to your code of conduct because this will seriously affect your sessions, and not only your success but that of your players! Do have one that, instead of being filled with don'ts, is filled with DO's! "What does this mean?" I hear you ask. Well, how many rules are filled with words such as don't bully, don't swear don't ....etc?

If you want to set out to create a positive coaching environment, a positive code of conduct is the first place to start! It sets the tone for the way in which you work and your expectations of the group. So many sessions have set 'rules'. I don't like that word because it makes me want to rebel already!

Sample Code of Conduct

- We always treat each other with respect and that includes coaches, players, other teams, all umpires and officials and anyone who we meet here at our sessions, and at all other times. This means we know that we are respected too.

- We know that we can always do more than we think possible, and that is why we always practise putting 100% effort into everything we do.

- We enjoy listening and learning, and so during demonstrations, when our coach speaks we listen and are quiet. If one of us speaks, our coach likes to hear, and we remain quiet for that to happen too.

- We like to communicate easily and have fun, so during practices we talk and offer each other feedback and encouragement willingly.

- We support each other at all times and this means that we are willing to work with any member of the group even if they are stronger or weaker than ourselves.

- To stay safe, we speak to our coach so they can acknowledge if we leave the sports-hall for any reason, and we heed any safety alerts from our coach at all times.

- We each accept responsibility for our own learning and that means we understand that we take out what we put in.

- We see ourselves as outstanding ambassadors of our sport, of our club and of ourselves, and we value ourselves highly because our actions reflect excellence in all things.

- We appreciate that the sessions belong to the players and our coaches support us. They help us set our goals and set us tasks to help us attain these. It is important therefore, for us to work as a team and to give feedback to our coaches, to help them deliver excellent training sessions.

Greet Athletes Individually at Every Session

Greeting athletes personally allows you to assess their energy levels, moods, and any old or new injuries, which means you will be able to meet their needs at that session. It also creates respect, builds a strong working relationship and a shared ownership of the session. At this stage, you may decide to change your session delivery to match the 'group mood' or to create higher or lower 'group' energy with the way you warm them up! This also makes sure you have spoken to every single child at least once personally during the session.

Get Your Group to Bond and Gel as a Team

Organise an ice breaker for the very first session of a brand new group. It helps build gelling, and aids group rapport. This means that learning takes place faster and easier. Ensure you get a 'buy in' at the start of coaching new players. Spend time with them whilst they fill out a questionnaire with enough details so you know how to motivate them and meet their needs. Let them understand how you work and what your expectations are at the outset.

Create opportunities within the coaching programme for team building exercises. These could be fun team games and leadership activities during the warm ups, Christmas parties, summer barbecues, family events and competitions, 24 hour marathons (a great way to raise money for your sessions and charities), end of competition trips to McDonalds etc

Create Winners and Leaders

Not every player who comes along to a coaching session is going to be a top national player or get selected for county matches; maybe they won't even particularly like the idea of entering any competitions or tournaments! However, they can ALL develop a WINNING ATTITUDE and this is vital for living life fully and getting the most out of everything we do! Acknowledge an individual's skills and talents and play to their strengths. If they show technical prowess use them as demonstrators.

If they have good communication skills get them to teach a new player a skill, such as movement patterns etc. If they are outgoing give them the task of 'befriending' newcomers. Shy children can be given tasks to help them become more confident, for instance taking the register or being a shuttle monitor etc.

Select captains to run the teams. I have found that using a shy player for this really helped them develop social skills, because they took on the responsibility of organising their team players, taking money etc. Allowing teams to be organised by the players themselves has always given my groups excellent results because matches become more important, players take ownership of results and the group gels strongly.

There is always a great deal of work to be done when working with groups and coaching. The more of this the coach delegates and shares, the more the group build their own skills and individuals develop self-worth, confidence, leadership skills and a winning attitude!

Praise Specifically and Honestly and Expect the Best

Acknowledging strengths builds strong foundation to work on developing weak areas! Always begin with an acknowledgement of what is going well; see the 'greatness' in each child. Always make reference to the 'behaviour or action' and not the person. Give all praise and corrections in private because it prevents any resentment within the group. Likewise, when questioning a child on any inappropriate behaviour, do it in private; there are two good reasons for doing so.

1. If you ask a question such as "What was the purpose of (action)?" it allows discussion and invites explanations, this means that it can be resolved easier.

2. By dealing with the issue quietly and calmly and in private, the child gets attention, but not group attention which means that you are creating a break in a pattern of

behaviour, because very often negative behaviour is to get attention from the group.

By expecting the best from every individual you will usually get good results. Remember that perception is projection and your group is merely a mirror of you the coach!

Be impeccable with your word! This means that when you speak, you use integrity and you only say what you mean! Sarcasm in a coaching session is out of place, out of order and is seen as 'bullying'!

Managing Behaviour

This is covered throughout the whole of this work in one way or another. It is worth remembering that all behaviour usually has a positive intention, it is learned and often becomes nothing more than a habit! A helpful belief to have is that PEOPLE are not their behaviours, so accept the person and change the behaviour.

It is all too easy to put people into 'boxes' and to 'label' them. Some parents can be heard admonishing a child saying "You bad boy". This directly labels the child as a behaviour! Separate the person from their behaviour because it allows you to see their potential. Learn to see the huge potential within people, see the great person they are behind their unhelpful behaviour. The more you practice this, the more likely you will be to help them develop their strengths.

EVERYONE is doing the best they can with the resources they have available. Behaviour is geared for adaptation and the present behaviour is the best choice available at the time, given the knowledge and experiences up to that point. Begin to accept that all behaviour is motivated by a positive intent. It might take some people a while to adopt this as a belief, but accepting it forms powerful results in every relationship. It is the basis of all forgiveness.

Give praise when positive behaviours are noticed, because you can begin to draw out more positive behaviours. When there is a disruptive or unhelpful behaviour that needs stopping, you could ask, "What is the purpose of doing that?" This focuses on the 'action' and allows the person to 'consider' their action. There is then the possibility for open discussion leading to finding different ways of behaving. Many children use inappropriate methods of seeking attention and you could help them to discover other ways of meeting their needs.

Many coaches and teachers miss the opportunity of teaching some important emotional- intelligence and life skills by simply admonishing unwanted behaviour. Instead, take the opportunity to look at the reasoning behind inappropriate behaviour and help your young people find more appropriate and effective ways of behaving!

Become an excellent communicator and role model. Make your coaching sessions interesting and enjoyable. Allow your athletes 'ownership' of learning and set a good pace and show high standards yourself, because then your players will be directed into positive behaviours and attitudes. It is wise to note that a coach has 'lost it!' if they have to 'shout' at their group. In fact, when a coach does shout in order to maintain order they have entered into the negative energy. A leader will have the 'authority' to become still and quiet because they know that their group will follow!

Sell Your Subject

When you go to buy a car, would you buy it without seeing it first? In fact, doesn't everyone want to see anything they buy first? You want to know the benefits too don't you? And so it is with learning! If you 'want' to learn, you will learn faster and enjoy it more wouldn't you agree? How does this apply to coaching?

Coaches all know the value of demonstrations but all too often some get caught up in the little details. They give out lots of information of 'how' to do something before the group are interested. There is no interest yet because the group don't have a clue of the benefits of doing 'it' and knowing what 'it' actually is and 'WHY' it's done!

What would the difference be if you could build anticipation and excitement first? Do you think your group would listen and take in more information?

Show them WHAT it is and WHY it benefits them to do it! This way you have grabbed their attention at the start, built anticipation and motivated them to want to learn how to do it! Only then do you go on to give just a few details and get them on their way to practice the skills.

GIVE REASONS. Use the word 'BECAUSE' a great deal when you are coaching if you want your athletes to do what you want them to do willingly.

The delivery of information is as important as the information itself; therefore, practice your delivery skills! A monotone voice, a small presence, poor posture, and inappropriate body language can bore a group; it lacks inspiration and motivational power. Instead, it encourages listlessness, a lack of attention and misbehaviour.

Excellence in communication and delivery is inspirational, motivational and enjoyable. Setting a good pace keeps the group's interest. Good delivery and communication skills accelerate learning because there is higher commitment. Enjoyable learning is easily remembered! Your personal development in the area of communication will provide great value to yourself and to your athletes.

Give Value

Your value as a coach ultimately depends on what you transfer to your players. What is the effect of your coaching on your group? What changes to their performance, attitude, beliefs, self-esteem, social skills, communications, occurs because YOU are their coach? It doesn't matter what qualifications and degrees you have. Your value is based on the perception of the receiver and whether you are meeting their needs and expectations. What impact do you have on your group? When you are aware of your value, you can focus on increasing it; by finding more ways to keep impacting more players, in faster time, and with progressively better results.

****

Activity:

How do you rate yourself on a scale of 1 to 5 where 1 is not at all or poor, and 5 always or excellent on the following:

1. Personal presentation
2. Get to know your athletes
3. Code of conduct
4. Greet athletes individually at every session
5. Get your group to bond and gel as a team
6. Create winners and leaders
7. Praise specifically and honestly, and expect the best
8. Managing behaviour
9. Sell your subject
10. Give value

Take a look at your scores and think about any areas you can improve which will have a positive effect on your athletes.

****

What action/s are you going to take?

....
....
....
....
....
....
....
....

"The aim of life is self-development. To realise one's nature perfectly - that is what each of us

is here for."

Oscar Wilde

"Most of us who aspire to be tops in our fields don't really consider the amount of work required to stay tops."

Althea Gibson

4

PERIPHERAL

VISION

"We're going to do the silent count, whatever we need to do. You've got to look at the ball, concentrate. As for looking at your guy, that's what peripheral vision is for."

David Diehl

Peripheral Vision is that part of your vision that detects objects outside of your direct field of view.

The coach's vision needs to take in a great deal of information, often from distances and involving many athletes at once. Not only are we observing them for the purposes of improving their performance, we also have the responsibility for their safety, seeing fair play, and noticing individuals within a large group; I'm sure you can think of many more reasons. Utilising peripheral vision enables the coach to broaden their focus and take in more information easily and effectively, indeed the athletes may come to think we actually have eyes in the back of our head!

****

Activity:

Look as far into the distance as possible: if you are indoors in a small room, then look out of the window. Remain looking out into the distance and while doing so, bring your hands up in front of your eyes at arms length with your index fingers pointing out and meeting each other. Your other fingers can remain folded back on the palm of your hands.

Now move your fingers apart and together again 2/3cm.

You should keep looking out into the distance past your fingers as you do this.

What do you notice?

If you noticed little floating sausages then you created a good peripheral vision.

You can test this out by creating peripheral vision again (by repeated practice you can achieve this without needing to use your fingers first) and bring your hands out to the side of your head at arm-length and still be able to see both of them.

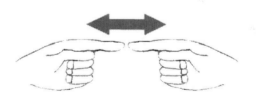

****

When you use good peripheral vision it enables you to take in the 'big picture' and still notice the things you as a coach need to observe carefully. It is very useful when observing beginners who may become nervous and consequently tighten their muscles if they think they are being observed or scrutinised by their coach!

Helping your athletes to use their peripheral vision means that they 'see' more of the game and for example, in the badminton context can watch the shuttle, see the spaces and be aware their partner and opponents positions.

****

Action:

What practices can you come up with to help your athletes improve their peripheral vision.

....

....

....

....

....

....

"He's good at finding guys out of his peripheral vision. Usually he can just get it and fire it, and you're not ready for it because you don't think he sees you. He's got awesome vision."

Ben Street

5

SENSORY ACUITY

"We cannot create observers by saying "observe," but by giving them the power and the means for this observation and these means are procured through education of the senses"
Maria Montessori

Using Peripheral Vision to observe people

Now you have been practicing and extending your peripheral vision, you have very probably noticed the benefits for yourself, and can get into peripheral vision easily at any time. You may be using it more often, not just for coaching but when walking, shopping, and many other times too perhaps.

What is Sensory Acuity?

Sensory Acuity is being able to notice the slightest change in someone's behaviour and emotion and is the first step to understanding athlete's behaviour. These changes can indicate how the person is feeling, reacting, and possibly thinking. It requires practice and knowledge to master sensory acuity.

Why might developing sensory acuity be helpful to us in our coaching?

Well, what would it be like to read peoples thoughts without them speaking? When we give our instructions wouldn't it be useful to know whether our athletes have understood them? Have you ever missed the critical signal that would have told you that you've gone just too far in an argument? Perhaps you have not been perceptive enough to notice the physiology, tone of voice or energy that indicates changes to another person's emotional state.

Paying Attention to Your Own Internal and External Signals

How often have you had a 'gut reaction' that said "No, don't do this!" or "Yes, this is what I really want to do!" and you ignored it and later regretted your action or inaction? Often, we do not pay sufficient attention to what is going on inside ourselves. Internal signals are physiological reactions that are always present and we frequently are just not aware of them. Maybe because we have ignored them for such a long time they are now out of our conscious awareness.

Some of the internal or physiological responses you could start paying attention to are:

- Holding your breath
- A tightening in your stomach or chest
- A certain pain or twitch
- A feeling of joy, love or accomplishment - or are these feelings you tend to ignore?
- Internal representations (images/sounds/etc.) you create in your mind.

I believe it is very important for me to understand what is going on inside of me. For example, there are two conversations happening at one time. The first is the one I have with myself and the second is the one that I have with you. If I do not feel good about myself, this will be demonstrated in my conversation with you through my choice of words, my tone of voice, my body language, and the energy coming from me. Even if you are not consciously aware of these signals coming from me, you will be at an unconscious level, and you will react to them in some way.

When observing other people, you will want to notice the following characteristics:

- Words they use
- Eye movements (eye accessing cues)
- Changes in skin colour/tone
- Breathing
- Voice quality
- Posture/gestures
- Changes in energy – going from motivated to lethargic.

The Blushing Scale
Are you Embarassed?

a little embarassed   really embarassed   extremely embarassed

It is so easy to notice a person blushing, where the neck and or face begin to glow red or crimson and there could be many different reasons for this couldn't there? Is this person embarrassed, angry, or just having a hot flush?

Below is a list of things to practice noticing when developing your sensory acuity in order to communicate well.

CHANGES OF

• Skin colour

• Breathing

• Lower Lip Size

• Eyes

BE AWARE!

It is very easy to make incorrect assumptions about someone's emotions. For example, anger and determination may generate similar external cues. I can think of one of my own athletes who doesn't smile, in fact he looks pretty fed up whether he is practicing or playing games. I often wonder why he attends the sessions! However, his mother repeatedly says that he really enjoys coming along!

CALIBRATION

Calibration is matching the **body language** to the description of the athlete's **emotion/word**. When we do this we need to take in as much information as we possibly can, and we do this by using all our own senses and 'feelings'.

In the first exercise below for example, we see something or someone we **dislike**, having different auditory cues to something or someone we **like**.

****

Activity:

Auditory Acuity:

Friend/Foe:

Identify which your friend is thinking of from the sounds. Stand back to back with your friend in a quiet room.

- Ask them to think of someone they dislike
- Let them build a strong impression of that person in their mind
- Now ask them to count aloud from 1 to 10
- Calibrate the 'sound' for foe
- Have your friend think of someone that they like
- Let them build a strong impression of that person in their mind
- Now ask them to count aloud from 1 to 10
- Calibrate the 'sound' for friend
- Now have your friend choose the person they 'like' or 'dislike'
- Ask them to count aloud from 1 to 10.
- Identify which is friend or foe by the different sounds.

****

Physiology is the primary way people communicate; 55% of communication is through our body language. This is a good reason to hone our observation skills and to notice the changes made through the body. When the body language doesn't match the words being spoken, take the meaning of the body language because this is the most accurate.

****

Activity

Postural observation:

Have a friend stand or sit in front of you.

- Observe and hold an image of that person
- Close your eyes
- Have your friend move an arm, a leg, tilt the head, etc.
- Open your eyes and identify how your friend has moved.

Repeat the exercise with less and less dramatic moves until you can recognise subtle changes like an eyebrow raised or minor head tilt.

****

Activity

Yes/No:

Ask your friend some closed questions that will make them respond with a 'Yes'.

- Are you alive?
- Are you awake?
- Is it daylight?
- Calibrate' their responses for 'Yes'

Ask your friend some closed questions that will make them respond with a 'No'.

- Can pigs fly?
- Are you dead?
- Can you hold your breath for an hour?
- Calibrate' their responses for 'No'
- Now ask closed questions without your friend responding verbally

- Identify your friend's response without them speaking.

****

As a coach you already know about the power of practice because you create practices for your athletes and encourage them to repeat them. You probably agree then, that all results are based upon the quality and repetition of practice.

In order to strengthen your sensory acuity skills, you may choose to do the practices above and you might even enjoy the results because you will discover more than you knew before.

ACTION:

Pay attention to your athletes' physiology, behaviour, voice etc. Calibrate their normal states so that you can tell when things are not going well for them. This is a useful skill and further on in this book we will be looking at ways of making changes. Your sensory acuity is important in influencing and creating change and when using visualisation with your athletes.

"He doesn't watch, he notices."

Thomas D'Evelyn

6

THE EFFECT OF VOICE ON BEHAVIOUR

"Words mean more than what is set down on paper; it takes the human voice to infuse them with shades of deeper meaning."

Maya Angelou

Why don't coaching courses spend any time on developing the coaching voice? As leaders and communicators we use our voices to deliver the words that will help our athletes to develop their sporting potential. Our most powerful tool to give instructions, excite interest, motivate, inspire, and to maintain excellent energy which underpins discipline and learning, is our voice.

If you listen in to an ordinary conversation between two people, in a bar or on a bus, and then imagine it on the stage, you know you wouldn't be able to hear it past the front row of the stalls, unless it was performed by competent actors. Although coaching is not precisely the same as acting, there are some similarities. In both professions it is necessary to be heard, to engage attention, and to transmit a message.

When you are coaching in sports halls you often have to contend with noisier sports, music, the movement and noise of others which distracts the group's attention and puts a strain on your vocal chords too. Your athletes may find it is too much effort to concentrate on your delivery, and with so much going on aurally, boredom may set in.

Have you ever listened to a speaker giving a speech, or someone reciting a long story, and their voice is so irritating that you focus more on the irritation of the voice, and completely miss what the speaker is actually saying? If a coach is unable to hold the group's attention with effective use of their voice, there will be repercussions on the group, leading to inappropriate behaviour. If a coach's voice comes across in a patronising way, or is monotone or weak, the coach may experience a loss of control of their group. On the other hand, effective coaching can also be hampered by coaches who constantly 'Bark out their orders' or shout! In fact there are many people who speak so loudly you actually find yourself stepping back a few paces; do you know anyone like that? When anyone is constantly being barked or shouted at, the brain filters out the sound which means that response is lessened! Many coaches have no idea about the effect of their voice on their athletes or, indeed, know what they do really sound like!

We listen to, and learn from a voice that sounds confident and has energy. We switch off from a voice that is strained, flat or just plain boring. It is therefore vital to consider how the voice is managed and cared for, especially when it is used professionally.

****

Activity:

Instant evaluation for your speaking voice exercise

Read the following passage out loud into a tape recorder or even on the voice recorder on your mobile phone. If you prefer, you can simply talk about the start of a typical day from getting up to leaving to go to work etc. Whatever you do, ensure you speak at least 8 or 9 full sentences.

Before now, I had never really paid much attention to the way I sounded. I would merely go about my day to day business, talking to people in a general way with no thought whatsoever. I would often stop to chat with friends in a supermarket and have a laugh with the neighbours as we passed each other as we went along our way.

Sometimes I would need to raise my voice, for example in a bar, having a drink with friends because I couldn't hear them and I suppose they wouldn't be able to hear me either come to think of it! Of course I love to tell stories to the children when they go to bed at night and it's not unusual for me to fall asleep before they do! This means that getting to the end of any story is a particular challenge!

****

Most of us generally have a sense of what we don't like about our voices, but we might find it difficult to put it into technical terms:

****

Activity:

Let's see how you did.

Play the tape back and at the same time look through the following list and mark the items that you think apply to you.

Did you:

Start strong but peter out by the end? Yes/No

Have to frequently clear your throat? Yes/No

Sound too soft? Yes/No

Notice that your voice felt too low and gravelly, especially at the ends of sentences? Yes/No

Hear your voice breaking in some parts? Yes/No

Sound nasal? Yes/No

Sound monotonous? Yes/No

Sound squeaky? Yes/No

Sound breathy? Yes No

****

Vocal Tips: - Use the passage you read before and tape yourself again as you practice these tips to improve your voice.

Speak while your stomach is coming in. Put your hand on your belly button and take a big breath in. As you speak allow your stomach to fall back in to its normal position.

Speak much louder if you are not shouting or too loud already! Simply pretend you are speaking to someone on the other side of a large room.

Join your words! Allow the words to flow from word to word with no blank spaces in between. Only stop the flow of words when you need to draw breath, or when you want to pause for emphasis.

When you play back the tape and listen again, you should notice a stronger more powerful and resonant sounding voice when you join your words allowing them to flow. Remember that pauses are extremely effective if they are in the right place! Allowing your words to flow cuts out the interference of the "ums" and "ah's" and can even help prevent stuttering! There is nothing worse than listening to someone who keeps putting too many spaces in at the wrong times and who separates every word. Start to listen more to how people talk, it's very interesting!

Voice Tone

"We often refuse to accept an idea merely because the tone of voice in which it has been expressed is unsympathetic to us."

Friedrich Nietzsche

Your tone of voice is closely linked to your facial expression. A frown on your face will make your voice sound harsh and cold. But a smile will warm up your voice, making it sound friendly and inviting.

In voice, there are three main kinds of tonality and inflection, this is when there is a change of pitch and these are shown below:

Questions – inflections are upwards

Statements –are an even tone, with no inflection

Commands – inflections are downwards

****

Activity:

Practice Saying the sentences above using only the word 'word' and using the inflection to hear the difference.

Question - eg "word word word"

Statement - e.g. "word word word"

Command - e.g. "word word word"

Be aware of how you give instructions to your group, how do you sound to others?

****

Make Statements, don't Ask Questions

Have you ever? Met someone? Who always sounds? Like they are asking questions? Even when they aren't? When your voice tone goes up at the end of a sentence it makes you sound unsure and insecure; instead, if you want to make a statement, use an even tone. When you want to give a command, focus on bringing your voice tone DOWN at the end of your sentences.

How many questions do you remember Darth Vader asking? Exactly!

Many coaches use questions instead of commands merely due to the inflection of their voice! An example of this is, "Can you all come over here please?" Have a go at saying this with a weak voice and an upward inflection! Now say it again using a strong voice with a downward inflection. Do you notice that even though the words are the same, and are polite and friendly, the responses will be quite different?

In any communicating situation the use of voice is as important as the actual content. How you say things, is as important as what you say. Actors and actresses spend time with voice coaches to develop greater dynamic ranges. When you listen to another person's voice you are literally bathed in sound from the speaker. When the "sound of the word" reflects or is congruent with the meaning of the word, you are more likely to remember what is said. For example the word "stretch" should sound like "streeeeetch" so the word sounds stretched rather than spoken in a clipped manner.

If you use congruent tonality along with speed and volume, you can be quickly and easily understood by your athletes. I have heard many trainee coaches saying "Run fast" with a flat, quiet and even slow tempo of their voice! Of course you can imagine the results for yourself.

How do you communicate: fast/slow, long/short, high/low? Are you effective? Have you recently listened to yourself and heard your cadence, speed, volume, pitch, tone and inflections? For my own personal development I have joined Toastmasters and have definitely benefitted from receiving excellent feedback, learnt many new skills and have become far more expert in my communication skills. Toastmasters International is available for anyone to join. There are groups all over the world and there's definitely one right near you.

For male coaches; you can get all the theoretical benefits of bodybuilding, increased status, more influence, and more attraction of the opposite sex, by simply improving your voice? Think about it. I'm sure you've met a man sometime in your life who was short, skinny or both and you somehow knew that this was a man of substance. He didn't look like a bouncer even though he looked confident with status.

This means that you can effectively send out the message, "I am strong, I am healthy, and I am virile," using **confident body language** and voice tone alone! Are you aware yet that improving your vocal delivery and body language could massively impact your communication and impact greatly on all your interactions?

The key points to effective vocal production are:

- Being aware of how you actually sound when coaching
- Using appropriate vocal variety - speed, tempo, volume and pitch

- Remembering that the sound of your voice conveys a bigger message than even your words!
- Your voice is a key component in having authority.

Remember:

1. Your voice has a direct impact on those who are listening to you
2. You can switch people on or turn them off by your vocal quality
3. Your voice creates an instant impression of who you might be.

"So I got home, and the phone was ringing. I picked it up, and said 'who's speaking please?' and a voice said 'You are'."

Tim Vine

"There is no index of character so sure as the voice."

Benjamin Disraeli

"A pleasant voice, which has to include clear enunciation, is not only attractive to those who hear it, its appeal is permanent."

Loreta Young

7

RAPPORT

"The most effective way to achieve right relations with any living-thing is to look for the best in it and then help that best into the fullest expression."

Allen Boone

Rapport is an ability or technique used to create good relationships and gain trust and confidence. As a coach you want people to have confidence in your abilities and trust that you know what you are doing. You are going to be taking your athletes out of their comfort zones and to do this effectively the athlete will need to follow your guidance. You will have dealings with other coaches, parents, committees, centre staff................. the list is endless! By building rapport, it is possible to create a bond of trust, a feeling of connection and empathy, and to communicate on an unconscious level to achieve outstanding results.

Rapport is one of the most important elements of human communication and unconscious interactions. It is about trust and responsiveness.

I have seen many coaches meet new people for the very first time and go straight into teaching, training or coaching them without attempting to develop any rapport whatsoever! As a result, there is a barrier between them to begin with, that may or may not come down later as they get to know each other better. However, I also see rapport being broken over and over again by clumsy communication skills, assumptions, lack of vocal variety and limited language and behaviour patterns. To build rapport you don't have to like the other person, nor agree with their view; merely understand them. By creating and using rapport in your coaching sessions, your learners will be more responsive to you, they will trust your teaching, and be open to new ideas.

Can anyone build rapport? The answer is that everyone can build rapport! If you have friends and good relationships, then you commonly use rapport to make them and keep them. We usually build or use rapport unconsciously, although experienced practitioners also use it consciously. You may know, or even be one of those who can strike up a conversation with complete strangers and be able to chat away for hours; or you may have heard people comment "Have I met you before?" If you are one of these then you are definitely using rapport effectively already! However, there are many people who don't build rapport and as a result have poor communication skills and therefore poor results in many contexts. So the question is.......... How can we learn to build rapport immediately, and on purpose?

The easiest way to build rapport is to be genuinely interested in the other person. Generally speaking, we like to talk about ourselves! So by giving the other person the opportunity to do this, we actually build their ego, allowing them begin to feel good, and let down their guard. This will be enhanced by asking open questions, showing responsive body posture yourself, such as nodding and smiling in agreement, and giving appropriate eye contact.

When you are coaching children, it is important to find out what interests them outside of your sport. Find out what makes them laugh, what motivates them, what they find easy or difficult etc. It is just like making a new friend, but you are building the blocks to generate a good working relationship in which the athlete is able to learn quickly and enjoy their learning.

Elements of Rapport

Rapport can be broken down into the following:

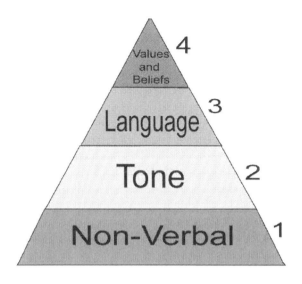

Level 1

This is the first level we communicate on. Think about communicating with a baby or someone with a different language. We use hands to express our words when language is a barrier and we rock the baby fast or slow to match their needs. Maybe you have experienced for yourself or seen a mother jigging a baby fast when the baby is crying frantically, and the slowing the jigging down to match as he/she calms down. Humans tend to respond to the non-verbal communication BEFORE the words; this means that if the actions don't match the words, it will be the action that is taken as the meaning.

Level 2

The tone of voice plays a massive part in communicating our messages. Start to notice changes of tone or pitch in yourself and others.

Level 3

We each have our own preferred representational style of language whether we prefer visual, auditory or kinaesthetic representation systems, and this is reflected in our choice of words. The representational systems are explained earlier. Practice listening carefully to discover the representational styles of the people you speak to.

Level 4

This is the highest level of rapport and occurs when you are actually matching your values and/or your beliefs with the person you are communicating with.

Top Tip: Notice how the other person shakes your hand on greeting. This personal touch is a powerful way to determine how receptive that person may be to building rapport and listening to your message. If, in initiating the handshake, you turn your hand outwards to the right very slightly and then, in the grasp, turn it slightly back to the left and they follow you with no resistance, they are open and receptive. This means they are going to be easier to teach.

We tend to be friends with people who are similar to us, or have similar interests. However, we don't need to be friends with everyone, and building rapport doesn't mean we have to be 'friends'. Achieving good levels of rapport is extremely powerful because communication is far more effective, giving excellent results.

Sales people are highly trained in rapport building because it develops trust and confidence from their clients towards themselves.

To build rapport we need to meet the other person at the 'place they are at, 'to join them in 'their model of the world'. To do this we can match or copy the actions exactly or we can mirror their actions. If we are mirroring them, when they raise their left hand we raise our right one. Matching is generally less obvious at least on the conscious scale. Once we have matched and/or mirrored, which is known as pacing, we can then lead, and the other person will follow. We are then in the position to influence!

As with all skills, we gain from good practice with plenty of repetition. Here then, are some practices that you can do, and once begun you will become aware of the resulting benefits.

****

Activity:

Practice building rapport

Step 1 PACING (matching and mirroring)

Do step 1 in subtle ways so as not to be noticed! There would be nothing more annoying than to feel someone copying you, and rapport would be broken!

1. Use you sensory acuity to notice, physiology, how are they sitting or standing, where is their weight, what is their posture?
2. Notice their voice pitch, tone, speed and volume. Match this carefully.
3. Notice the words that are being used, do they represent visual, auditory or kinaesthetic preferences – and match these closely.

Step 2 (Leading)

Once you think you are in rapport, begin to lead by shifting position, putting your hand to your face, crossing or uncrossing legs etc. Notice whether the other person does the same, if they do, then you definitely have rapport going because they are now following your lead.

****

When you are in public places, be observant and notice who is in rapport around you. How many people can you get into rapport with, even from a distance?

Dealing with Autopilot Resistance

Most people spend most of their time on Autopilot! This is when we are not being fully conscious of what is happening around us. If your players come into your session in this state, they are unlikely to take on board and remember what you are teaching.

Many tasks we perform are so familiar to us that we perform them unconsciously, without thinking about them. Can you remember how many times you have driven your car on a familiar journey or road, and have no recollection of passing certain traffic lights or making certain turns? Or if you don't drive, how many occasions have you become aware that you have walked or, carried out familiar tasks with absolutely no memory of actually doing so?

This is commonly known as autopilot behaviour. This is a trance state whereby we are being driven by our subconscious. It is broken when something out of the ordinary happens. For example, this could be avoiding a sudden obstacle on the road in front of us and this jolts us back to full consciousness.

Many of our memories are locked up in our subconscious, and these are unavailable to our conscious mind. This means that we have no conscious memory of anything that happens when our subconscious is driving us on autopilot. The implication of this is that learners may not remember the lesson because they are not consciously aware.

Anything that is out of our normal routine breaks us out of autopilot and is remembered consciously. So in order to make an impact upon someone, and be remembered, we need to bypass their autopilot.

Look for the kind of questions and statements that the other person would normally receive from people while in a given situation, and then use a very different sort of question or statement! Good questioning has the effect of knocking people out of their autopilot. It gets them to notice and interact fully and consciously with you because you have created stronger rapport, and they see or feel that you are interested in them.

Some examples:

At a supermarket checkout, how many customers go through without acknowledging the person at their till? The tiller is probably on autopilot. What could you say to the tiller to break their trance? And what might the affect be? Could we get better service or simply enhance their day?

When purchasing a large item that is high cost such as a car, an example of a 'normal' opening from a customer might be, "I am interested in buying 'XYC', what can you tell me about it?" This would merely trigger a pre-programmed response from the salesperson. However, if you can change your approach enough for example: "You know what? I know you'll probably want to sell me this 'xyc' anyway, but I have already researched it, so tell me, in your honest opinion how does it compare to the 'xxxxxx version'?"

This approach, where you have identified with him by using the word 'know', may jolt him out of his autopilot which means he will be more likely to be honest with you than he would otherwise have been.

So, how can this jolting out of autopilot be useful to you as a coach? Well, by breaking autopilot to a new athlete or group means you establish a quicker rapport, marks you out as a different sort of coach to 'other coaches', and helps people remember you easily.

****

Activity:

Practice breaking autopilot

Purposefully approach someone who would usually give you an autopilot response when you speak to them. Use a statement that is very different to anything they'd expect and see how successful you are in establishing rapport with that person. Some good examples of people you could choose to practice on are members of the opposite sex in a social setting (be very careful!), salespeople, shopkeepers, door to door collectors, strangers in a queue.

****

Remember:

- Building Rapport helps to build trust
- Being in Rapport creates more opportunity to influence the other person
- Being CONSCIOUS of what you are doing means coming out of your own auto-pilot state.

"For most women, the language of conversation is primarily a language of rapport: a way of establishing connections and negotiating relationships."

Deborah Tannen

"I like her because she smiles at me and means it".

Anonymous

8

REPRESENTATION SYSTEMS

"Language is the means of getting an idea from my brain into yours without surgery."

Mark Amidon

People are born into a culture, a set of rules, and a language system to identify everything within our world including them-selves.

We experience and learn about our world through our representation systems which are, our five senses; visual (seeing) auditory (hearing), kinaesthetic (touch and feelings), gustatory (taste) and olfactory (smell). We are going to concentrate on the main three of visual

(V), auditory (A) and kinaesthetic (K) and we each have our preferred representational system or sense in different contexts. To excel at communication it is useful if we recognise our preferred system and are able to change it to match the people we wish to influence. When speaking to groups it is very useful to use a mixture rich with references from all systems because it helps create greater rapport and helps the individuals within the group understand your message easier.

Here is a preference test to help you discover your most favoured system.

Instructions:

For each of the following statements, assign a number to every phrase. Use the following system to indicate your preferences:

1- Least descriptive of you

3 - Next best description

3 - Next best description

4 - Best description of you

If you have trouble deciding between two phases, go with your first thought

1 When on vacation at the beach, the first thing that makes me glad to be there is:

A. The feel of the cool sand, the warm sun or the fresh breeze on my face

B. The roar of the waves, the whistling wind or the sound of birds in the distance

C. This is the type of vacation that makes sense or the cost is reasonable

D. The scenery, the bright sun, and the blue water

2. When I feel overwhelmed, I find it helps if:

A. I can see the big picture

B. I can talk or listen to another person

C. I can get in touch with what is happening

D. I make sense of things in my head

3. When given an assignment at work, it is easier to carry out if:

A. I can picture what is required

B. I have a feeling for what is happening

C. I have an understanding of what is required

D. Someone talks to me about what is required

4. I find it easier to follow a presentation if:

A. I feel in touch with the presenter and the material is within my grasp

B. There is a visual display so that I can visualise the concepts

C. The presentation is based on facts and figures and is logically presented

D. The presenter speaks clearly with varying tonality or uses sound to emphasise the message

5. When buying a car, I make my decision on:

A. The purchase price, petrol mileage, safety features, etc
B. How comfortable the seats are or the feeling I get when I test drive it
C. The colour, styling or how I would look in it
D. The sound of the engine or stereo system or how quiet it rides

6. I communicate my thoughts through:

A. My tone of voice
B. My words
C. My appearance
D. My feelings

7. When I am anxious, the first thing that happens is:

A. Things begin to sound different

B. Things begin to feel different

C. Things begin to look different

D. Things begin to not make sense

8. During a discussion, I am most influenced by:

A. The other person's logic

B. The other person's tone of voice

C. The energy I feel from the other person

D. Seeing the other person's body language or being able to picture the other person's viewpoint

9. I assess how well I am doing at work based on:

A. My understanding of what needs to be done

B. How I see myself making progress

C. The tone of voice used by my colleagues and superiors

D. How satisfied I feel

10. One of my strengths is my ability to:

A. Select what needs to be done

B. Make sense of new facts and data

C. Hear what sounds right

D. Get in touch with my gut feelings

11. It is easiest for me to:

A. Select the volume, base and treble for easy listening on a stereo system

B. Select an intellectually relevant point in a conversation

C. Select comfortable furniture

D. Select rich, attractive colour combinations

12. If you agree with someone, are you more likely to say:

    A. That feels right

    B. That looks right

    C. That sounds right

    D. That makes sense.

Representation System test results

Step One: For each question on the questionnaire, note your answers in the box with the appropriate letter. In other words if you gave 1D 4 points, then you would write 4 where the D is on question 1 (visual). Repeat for EVERY answer.

Step Two: Add the numbers associated with each Representational System.

Step Three: The comparison of the total scores in each column will give the relative preference for each of the four major Representational Systems

Question Number	Visual	Auditory	Kinaesthetic	Auditory Digital
1	D	B	A	C
2	A	B	C	D
3	A	D	B	C
4	B	D	A	C
5	C	D	B	A
6	C	A	D	B
7	C	A	B	D
8	D	B	C	A
9	B	C	D	A
10	A	C	D	B
11	D	A	C	B
12	B	C	A	D
TOTAL	V=	A=	K=	A$_d$=

What do these results mean to you? Let's find out.

VISUAL: Memorise by seeing pictures and are less distracted by noise. Often have trouble remembering and are bored by long verbal instructions because their mind may wander. They are interested by how the program looks.

AUDITORY: Typically are easily distracted by noise. They can repeat things back to you easily and learn by listening. They like music and like to talk on the phone. Tone of voice and the words used can be important.

KINAESTHETIC: Often they talk slowly and breathily. They respond to physical rewards and touching. They memorise by doing or walking through something. They will be interested in a programme that feels right or gives them a gut feeling.

UNSPECIFIED AUDITORY DIGITAL: They spend a fair amount of time talking to themselves. They memorise by steps, procedures, sequences. They will want to know the programme makes sense. They can also sometimes exhibit characteristics of other rep. Systems

Now that you have an idea of your personal favoured representational system, you may become more aware of the type of words you commonly use that so far you have used unconsciously. By very carefully listening to how other people speak, you can train yourself to listen out for the type of words they are using and therefore identify their personal Rep system too! What are the benefits of doing this? How many ways can this help you in your coaching – especially when coaching an individual?

VISUAL: See, Look, View, Appear, Show, Dawn, Reveal, Envision, Illuminate, Imagine, Clear, Foggy, Focussed, Hazy, Crystal, Picture.

AUDITORY: Hear, Listen, Sound(s), Make music, Harmonise, Tune in/out, Be all ears, Rings a bell, Silence, Be heard, Resonate, Deaf, Mellifluous, Dissonance, Question, Unhearing.

KINAESTHETIC: Feel, Touch, Grasp, Get hold of, Slip through, Catch on, Tap into, Make contact, Throw out, Turn around, Hard, Unfeeling, Concrete, Scrape, Get a handle, Solid.

UNSPECIFIED AUDITORY DIGITAL: Sense, Experience, Understand, Think, Learn, Process, Decide, Motivate, Consider, Change, Perceive, Insensitive, Distinct, Conceive, Know.

How can we best use these systems in coaching? Well, in badminton we might be teaching some basic footwork patterns and these are the kind of words we might use for teaching some basic footwork patterns.

VISUAL: Have a look as I show you a demonstration and at the same time, picture yourself doing the same.

AUDITORY: If you listen as I demonstrate you will hear a rhythm that will resonate with you and that you will be able to imitate.

KINAESTHETIC: As I step out on court and slip into some movement patterns you will grasp how easy it is, and get a handle on learning this method.

AUDITORY DIGITAL: I'm going to go through the process of moving so that you can understand the concept and then experience it for yourselves.

****

Activity:

Being creative and extending language.

1. Think of your own sport and a specific element that you coach, and then write one sentence that you might use in your every day coaching sessions in order to teach this element. At the same time focus on words explicit for each of the representational systems:

   Visual:...

   ....

   Auditory:...

   ....

   Kinaesthetic:...

   ....

   Auditory Digital: ....

2. Now think of a couple of sentences for the same coaching element that uses a cross section of words from each of the systems

   ....

   ....

....

....

....

The more you practice the easier it is to use a variety of predicates and not to stick to your own style. If you can now add another 50 sentences that you could use either in your sporting capacity or at home you will become fluent in these skills which will make you an advanced communicator, who finds persuasion easy.

****

Extending your range of language patterns and matching them to those you wish to communicate with, means that you are going to be understood more often. You will also create empathy which you will see later when you take a look at and tune into how you Build Rapport which will help you get a grasp of and understand good communication even more.

How our Internal Representation System Preferences can affect our relationships.

A man who is mainly visual may enjoy a neat tidy home, in fact neatness may mean a great deal to him and his feeling of well-being. You may know someone like this; everything sparkling clean, in its right place, clean sheets that are possibly ironed and the bed always made perfectly. He takes pride and care in his appearance and often judges others on their appearance.

What if he marries a woman who has a predominantly kinaesthetic internal representation system? She likes to feel comfortable and enjoys lots of cushions and soft furnishings. She never, or hardly ever notices a mess, she measures her home by the way she feels. This woman likes to feel comfortable and may tend to dress in a relaxed manner, or not bother much about her appearance.

You might already be aware what might happen as the years pass and the couple relaxes into their preferred styles more and more. The husband becomes irritated by dirty cups left where they had last been used, dust accumulating on carpets that hadn't seen the vacuum cleaner for a week, the dust settling on once shiny surfaces and the kitchen surfaces hardly ever seen at all as they hide beneath layers of plates waiting to visit the sink. When he complains of how he sees things he can't understand why she can't see his point of view!

It appears to him that things at home are becoming very unclear, and he is unhappy.

The communication between the couple is poor and relationships are strained!

When the husband completes an NLP course he suddenly realises where HE has been going wrong!

When he gets home, he says with good vocal tone and positive body language, "If I bring you some toast and tea in bed and it is warm and the bed is warm, and you are able to relax back on soft pillows as you enjoy eating, and feeling the comfort of the silky duvet brushing your skin when you change position becoming more relaxed." (She's recreating the words in her internal representation system and can probably actually feel the whole thing!)

He carries on speaking, - "And then as you snuggle in, you notice hard crusty crumbs all over the sheets and no matter where you move the crumbs stick into your flesh, irritating you to ...." By this time his wife pleads for him to stop and that he has completely ruined the whole 'picture'!! And the husband continues..........................."This is just an example of how I feel when I see cups left on the side unwashed and the house completely cluttered with mess!"

The wife is now able to 'see' her husband's point of view and the couple are able to compromise because the communication channels have been opened.

You might notice an awareness of how powerful it is to learn about representational systems; you may also wish to know how this learning can be applied to your coaching sessions as well as ordinary living. So let's move even deeper into the world of language and representation systems.

"Words have a magical power. They can bring either the greatest happiness or deepest despair; they can transfer knowledge from teacher to student; words enable the orator to sway his audience and dictate its decisions. Words are capable of arousing the strongest emotions and prompting all men's actions."

Sigmund Freud

9

GOING IN A LITTLE DEEPER

*"Words do not have a transpersonal truth; they
do not exist at all until and unless a human
being comes along and converts the word into
an internal representation."*

Dr Silvia Hartman

The abc's of the unconscious mind

How would you like to communicate effectively
if it was really easy to do? NLP states that the
alphabet of our communication system is the
same as our three main sensory systems, VAK.

We interface with the outside world by seeing, hearing and feeling, but we also experience things internally through the same systems.

VISUAL: As you are reading this page and seeing these words – you are also able to see or visualise inside your mind's eye. For example, you can easily bring up a picture in your mind's eye, of your kitchen, or bedroom, or if you read the word car, it's pretty likely that you conjure up some sort of image of a car too.

AUDITORY: As you sit there reading this page you might be hearing the tap dripping, noises in the next room or become aware of sounds you haven't noticed until now. At the same time you can become aware of your own internal dialogue, that voice that speaks to you constantly, and is so easy to recognise.

KINAESTHETIC: As you sit or stand reading this page, you can probably feel the chair or ground beneath you and the warmth or coolness of your surroundings. At the same time you could become aware of internal feelings such as swallowing, or a clearing of the throat, maybe your stomach gurgling or sensations of aches or discomfort that cause you to unconsciously move parts of your body.

Communication exists at two levels, external, that which we can hear, see and feel, and internal which is the unconscious level. This is different for each of us, and depends on our experiences, values and beliefs.

Words affect the unconscious or internal part of your representation system and everyone interprets their own meaning. Therefore, the meaning of communication is the response you get.

Every time you speak, the receiver makes pictures in their own minds eye. The pictures are based on the values, memories, beliefs and imagination of that person, and the picture and the meaning they create may not always match yours.

****

Activity:

Exploring some responses:

Have fun experimenting on creating pictures in your friend's mind's eye by asking the same questions to several friends and seeing the variety of answers!

1) "As I say the word 'Rose', what do you see in your mind's eye?"
   "What colour is it?"
2) "Now take a phrase – The woman looked into the shop window".

"What did the woman look like?"

"What sort of shop was she looking into?"

"Why was the woman there?"

You might want to choose some words and sentences of your own to play with now!

****

I wonder how many different answers you had with those simple questions.

With question 1, a simple object creates an image in the mind's eye, and this image depends on one's personal experience. Some people might see a bunch of roses, others a bed of roses or a single yellow rose, etc. Saying 'a single red rose', is more specific and more likely to get similar results from a range of people, although even here there could be other responses because I haven't stated what size, have I?

A simple phrase such as question 2, can also be interpreted in a variety of ways. If we had in front of us a table with some objects placed upon it, we could all agree on the size and dimension of the table because we can see the table, touch the table and measure the table. All these examples are dealing with objects from the material world; however, communicating some ideas can be far more complicated than these.

If I say "Holiday", what does this conjure up in your mind's eye? Your idea of an ideal holiday would probably be very different from mine and other peoples! The word holiday is a noun and yet 'holiday' is not a thing; rather it is an experience, or a concept that is not tangible and therefore doesn't belong in the 'material world'. Other examples of these types of 'words or concepts' are: 'love' 'romance' 'a relaxing evening'. These are words that describe nouns which don't actually exist in a physical sense, and they need extra clarification when you are communicating.

Imagine a sign that says 'Keep Off The Grass'; in your mind's eye, where do you see that sign? What do you see around the sign? Did you answer grass? This is the most common response. A sign saying 'Keep Off The Grass' is sending out a message of grass isn't it? If I am asking you to keep off the grass, what do I want you to do instead? Probably keep to the paths. Instead of stating 'Keep Off The Grass', I would suggest that a sign saying 'Keep To The Path' would be more effective for the unconscious mind to deal with.

Be aware of your internal images when you speak and realise that the people you speak to are normally prone to interpret and make different pictures and meanings. Select words carefully to enable you to influence the images you create inside your audience. Be specific when giving instructions so they are understood with the meaning you intended.

So, can you see that most people create images in their head according to the words they use?

Is creating images the only way we interpret communication, or is there more to learn that helps us communicate effectively with our athletes?

Mothers create a meaning from the burbling of their baby's chatter and usually respond with smiles, encouragement and praise to their offspring. This allows the infant to communicate and form language patterns as a partner in conversation. As the mother makes sense of her baby's burbles and behaviours, she offers her meaning to her child and suggests identities, world meanings and intentions. In fact she is programming into the child, beliefs about the child's identity and the world. These beliefs soon become the reality for the child. The way a mother and others respond to the child forms the basis of how a child sees itself in relation to others and how it expects to be treated, its language patterns and other social interactions.

As we grow up it is very easy to create our own meaning about other people and events from what we hear and see. We can imagine and assume meanings that are absolutely incorrect at times! How often can a relationship go wrong because of these misunderstandings? For example it has been known that when a husband hands a bouquet of flowers to his wife unexpectedly, she may question the motive behind it! "What do you want?" "What have you done wrong?" In fact, I confess that I may have been guilty of this myself at times! In some cases these responses may be more common than the thoughts "Oh he is showing how much he loves me", or "He is so considerate to think of surprising me like this".

Have you ever wondered why some athletes are less confident in certain situations? Why do some players become excessively angry at the smallest incorrect line call? What causes your athletes to perform uncharacteristically in specific venues, or against particular opponents? What would it be like if you could begin to understand what causes these negative behaviours and were able to make changes to behaviour and performance?

NLP Communication Model

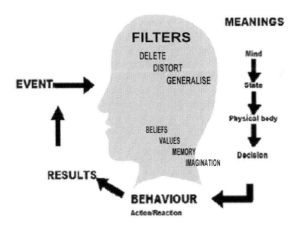

The NLP communication model helps to explain how we interpret meaning from events.

Learning this model allows you to begin the process of understanding people's differences. It shows how the mind and body are linked and how thoughts become behaviours. Being sympathetically aware of these concepts enables you to become more tolerant and start to redirect behaviours, attitudes and beliefs gently, intentionally and effectively for more positive outcomes.

The diagram of the NLP communications model is a brief introduction to the basics of how we construct our model of the world. When an event happens, we witness it through our five senses (VAKOG) and create our version of the event using a map of our values, memories, and beliefs; all of which may delete, distort and generalise the available information. Having done this, we create our own meaning of the event. We think of the meaning, which creates some sort of emotion. Emotion creates a physical change to our body and we make some sort of decision. That decision causes us to act or react in some way, and this gives us a result!

Our events are often the result of our actions. This is how we get caught in a loop of behavioural patterns! The difficulty for many people is that they don't understand that what they think is reality, is merely their own version of it. It is important to remember that "The map is not the terrain" and how we see things is usually incomplete and often wrong!

An event is filtered by deleting, distorting and generalising in the following ways.

DELETE: This is when we are omitting data or selectively paying attention to certain of our experiences and not others. Think of a time when you were so engaged in a conversation with someone that you were unaware of other events going on around you. With over 2million bits of data per second, your brain would be overloaded without filters.

DISTORT: Distortions can be made in seeing, hearing, or feeling things that are not really there. For an example, seeing someone you know in a crowd, but realising they are a stranger as they get closer. However, using distortion allows us to recognise a person again even when they are wearing completely different clothes. Distortion is common in language; for example: "He makes me angry." "You make me feel so small." "She makes me happy." All of these statements are evidence that the user has surrendered choice to other people or circumstances, and become a victim of their environment. Another distortion example is presumptions. Presumptions are when we presume something about another person with no evidence whatsoever! For instance, "I know you said that to hurt me!" "You're angry, I can tell." And another scenario could be, "I folded my arms because I am cold but you think I am unfriendly". Lastly, distortion by the means of interpretation, "I know I'm boring you because you are yawning!" The other person could merely be tired. Or, "I know you're angry because you're raising your voice." The other person may simply be excited, or feeling they need to speak louder to overcome background noise that they are aware of.

GENERALISE: Generalising is a way of drawing a conclusion about someone, or something, or an event based on only a few past experiences. For instance, we may say "He's always late" even though his lateness might occur solely in one context or only on a few occasions, therefore not actually true all the time. How often do you hear comments such as "All Germans put their towels on chairs early!" "Americans are loud!" All these comments are simply generalisations and cannot be true of every person. However, generalisations can be very useful. Familiarity with a chair means that we recognise many different types of chair/stool/sofa as something to sit on. Generalisations can then, make our life easier if we use them correctly.

VALUES: Values are a filter through which we decide what is good or bad and how we feel about our actions. We all have different models of the world and our values are based on these. When you communicate with yourself, or with other people, and your values don't match, there are going to be conflicts. Values are context related and what you want in a personal relationship could be very different to what you want in a business relationship.

BELIEFS: Beliefs are not necessarily based upon a logical framework of ideas and are unresponsive to logic. They are not intended to coincide with reality. Since you don't really know what is real, you have to form a belief-a matter of faith."

Beliefs are formed from a series of decisions which lead to a strong presumption; commonly known as a belief! Beliefs form the rules about what we think we can and cannot do.

MEMORIES: Memories filter your current reality. The way you remember things shows what values and beliefs are valuable for you at that time and yet memories are not necessarily true. The way you remember things will not be the same as someone else's memory of the event. Past experiences filtered in your unique way, have repercussions on how you view certain activities today. Some psychologists believe that as we age, our reactions to present external events have little to do with the present and are simply reactions to Gestalts. A gestalt is a number of similar memories grouped together.

IMAGINATION: Imagination involves forming a mental image of something that is not necessarily related to one's past experience, nor in the present environment. It allows you to be creative, to look to the future and to dream and plan. The brain does not recognise any difference between what is real and what is imagined, so imagination is a powerful tool for creating desired outcomes.

The next page shows a table with an example of a single sporting event. It demonstrates how one event can have different responses, depending on the values, beliefs and memories of the person experiencing it.

Sporting example:

The EVENT - A player has worked hard and arrived at the finals of the biggest tournament of his career, and during the deciding rally that determines the winner, he trips and sprains his ankle. He is forced to withdraw from the competition. He has now lost and is runner up.		
PLAYER A	**PLAYER B**	**PLAYER C**
POSSIBLE MEANINGS (thoughts)		
If I hadn't tripped, I could probably have won, so I know I can do it next time.	This is always happening to me – life is so unfair!	That F**********G S****** just cost me my win making me trip like that!!!
POSSIBLE EMOTIONAL STATES		
Calm	Disappointment	Anger
POSSIBLE PHYSIOLOGICAL CHANGES		
Muscles are relaxed, (apart from the painful area), breathing is steady.	Possibly floods of tears, a bending or drooping of the shoulders, head bowed looking downwards. Crying can produce increased heart rate, sweating and slowed breathing according to scientific studies.	Stress hormones (adrenaline and noradrenalin) are released. Heart rate climbs; an angry person's body releases chemicals to coagulate (clot) the blood, creating a situation that's potentially dangerous. Although there is no physical injury, the clot is formed, which can travel through the blood. Muscles tighten, face and neck flush . . . .
POSSIBLE DECISIONS		
Acceptance	I am upset and sulky	I am Angry
POSSIBLE BEHAVIOURS Actions/Reactions		
Smiles and waves to the crowd managing to sign a few autographs as he is taken off on a stretcher.	Sulking and hiding from people not wanting to speak.	Angry, swearing smashes the racket and breaks his hand as he punches it into the hard surface before he is taken off on the stretcher.
SOME POSSIBLE RESULTS (of the actions)		
Gets a standing ovation from his fans, and gains popularity. He is welcomed as a hero by the hospital staff and they fall over backwards to make his visit comfortable.	People don't know how to respond and shy away from him. He loses popularity and his fans are embarrassed for him. The hospital staff try to comfort him but soon give up and leave him all alone.	The Umpire penalises his poor behaviour, and he is restrained by officials all the way to the hospital where he is almost refused treatment because of his continuing aggressive manner.
The start of the event to the possible behaviours can happen so quickly it is hard to define whether the thoughts/states, physiological changes and decisions are simultaneous.		
What memories/values/beliefs could possibly attribute to the athletes creating these meanings and behaviour patterns?		
Has a sense of self- worth, confidence and self-esteem probably through positive parenting, and experiences/memories, and a secure childhood and maybe a natural positive personality.	Has not learned how to control emotions; possibly has memories of being left out of activities by friends/siblings. Could have learned that crying and sulking works by parenting methods.	Has learnt how to do anger, maybe has learnt to get his own way through the use of anger by modelling behaviours from parents. Possibly had weak parenting – parents who gave way easily to early temper tantrums. Possibly a natural 'Blamer' archetype personality

Understanding how each person behaves according to their experiences, values and beliefs leads to tolerance. It enables us to understand that we are able to separate the person from their behaviour.

In sporting terms when an athlete is 'being difficult', 'not listening', 'seems moody' or appears to be 'challenging in any way, it is easy for anyone to make presumptions that the athlete is simply behaving badly. On the other hand, you can presume that a person is not their behaviour; therefore, you can accept the person and change the behaviour. After all, isn't everyone doing the best they can with the resources they have available, and doesn't all behaviour have a positive intent?

Remember:

- When you speak, the other person makes their own interpretation of what you are saying
- When other people speak, you are likely to be making your OWN meaning of their words

- Everyone responds to events in different ways according to their own model of the world

- To begin to understand someone's behaviour, it is important to understand how they model their world.

Action:

- Think carefully when speaking. Choose words that are specific when you give instructions. Use questions to make sure that the listener understands your message.

- When listening, be aware of your voice in your head making your own interpretations. Turn this voice off! Listen fully to the speaker. Make sure you are taking on the meaning that the speaker is intending. Ask questions to ensure you really do understand.

"We do not see things as they are. We see them as we are."

The Talmud

10

PROGRAMMING

FOR SUCCESS

"The spirit, the will to win, and the will to excel are the things that endure. These qualities are so much more important than the events that occur."

Vince Lombardi

From what you have read thus far, you should now be aware that your communication has a direct effect on the receiver and that everyone creates a personal meaning based on their own values, beliefs, memories, and attitudes. Wouldn't it be great to use this knowledge to programme your players or athletes for success?

Practice Saying What you Want

Because you understand the process to create images in your athletes mind, you are can begin to apply the process deliberately.

Instead of putting either harmful or helpful images into some-one's mind, unintentionally, you can now use your awareness to speak with intent to help an individual develop positive images in their mind's eye which empowers them and aids success and achievement.

When you give your athletes instructions, what do you say? Do you tell them what not to do, or do you focus on telling them what you do want them to do? What images are you painting in their unconscious mind? Is it one of doing something well or are you conveying a hazy picture with mixed messages which their brain is now attempting to sort out? This is the reason it takes some sportspeople a long time to 'get the hang' of something, 'see' what is expected of them; or 'hear' the message correctly! Success for the athlete depends on the communication skills of the coach! This means that you should use precise words to affect the internal representation system, in other words, use language to convey the meaning you want to give that enables your athletes to be successful in their learning.

Can you just stop now and don't think of a yellow elephant?

I thought I told you NOT to think of one! I bet you did think of one though! Perhaps I should have said think of a Polar Bear; that way an elephant would never have entered your mind! The unconscious mind doesn't process the word 'don't' too easily! How many times can you remember being told NOT to touch and so you absolutely had to reach out and maybe with one finger just have that little poke, just to see (or should I say feel). I know I find it irresistible, maybe it is the 'mis-matcher' in me!

I see many coaches using the 'elephant approach' in their coaching and especially when giving feedback. They spend valuable time reinforcing poor technique by showing the player what they are doing wrong over and over again!

I often see coaches give out more than three instructions and EVERY instruction is telling the athlete what they SHOULDN'T be doing! When I brought this to the attention of a culprit on a training day, they argued that their communication had been extremely clear! However, they had not stated one positive instruction, nor even shown the athlete the correct technique that should be used! The brain has enough to cope with when learning new skills! The athlete in question had to take time to work out what was wanted and which bits to eliminate! Saying only what you want, accelerates learning and reinforces good techniques/learning. Be aware of how and what you communicate. Practice saying what you DO want someone to do!

Most people, including coaches use their words and voice unconsciously, and are unaware of their effects. The excellent communicator uses words and voice with intention; they know the impact their words and tone of voice can have, and use these to influence others in positive ways! Coaches who understand and utilise good language patterns, influence their players in positive ways to help them achieve their goals, build strong positive beliefs, good self-esteem and confidence.

Let's take a look at some common words and how they can be interpreted by the unconscious mind:

Don't

Asking someone not to do something makes them think about the thing you don't want them to do, which paradoxically makes them more likely to do it!

So say it how you want it to be, use positive language.

For example rather than say, "Don't swing your arm back", say instead, "Keep your arm in front". Rather than say "Don't hold your grip tight", say instead "Keep your grip soft".

Some athletes you work with like to do the opposite. These are called 'mis-matcher' types of personalities because when we say "Don't", they Do!

****

Activity:

Experiment using the word 'Don't'.

When a friend or a child is sitting down, say "Don't sit down".

Watch them and you will see a look of confusion and a delay whilst they work out what you mean! Isn't it easier to say "Stand up?"

Alternatively say "Don't" to some random act you see a friend doing – are the results still the same?

****

I have worked with a fellow assessor who, although charming, respectful, a thoroughly nice person and entirely professional, prepared the candidates for their assessment day with "Don't Worry!" These words were repeated constantly throughout the day! What message is being given? Is this the message intended by the assessor? What would you be saying instead?

Try

"Do, or do not... there is no try." ~Yoda, Star Wars

'Try' implies something will be difficult and you will not succeed. It can of course also be used as an alternative to 'experienced', as in "Have you tried bungee jumping?" The unconscious mind usually accepts the definition of failure, therefore 'try' should be used carefully and sparingly!

Compare: "We will try to do our best." with "We will do our best."

How many times do I hear coaches tell their athletes to 'try' to do something? Admittedly, 'try' is used more often by some than by others but, some coaches use it almost EVERY TIME they give an instruction. If you ask a player to play in a match, and they reply they would try to, are you confident that they will show up? How many times have you personally said "I'll try to come along."? And of course perhaps you just didn't have the time to consider the question fully before answering, or maybe you just didn't like to say no straight out!!

The word 'Try' is a ticket to mediocrity/failure/lack of effort!

If you really want to programme players and athletes for success then use clean language to express your intentions and give a very clear message that they 'will' do the practice. There should be no thought of failure, because you should be designing activities that are achievable yet still challenging.

But

'But' is a deletion word and deletes the sentence before! If you think about it we are conditioned to expect this, aren't we? How often can you remember waiting to hear 'But' when someone has offered you praise? 'However' and 'Although' have the same effect as 'But', i.e. "You played really well today, however there are a couple of areas we need to look at."

Using 'And' adds to what has just been said, so you could say, "You played really well today, and there are a few areas we can look at for next time.

Turn a sentence around by giving a development area first and then use 'But'. This erases the first statement and replaces it with a positive one.

Here is an example of turning a sentence round for a player losing a tournament match:

"I agree that you didn't get the result you wanted. The issue isn't that you lost this tournament, but how excellently you have played in all your last three tournaments. You have trained hard, learned lots of new skills and have gained respect from your opponents, team mates and coaches. After we go over some of the tactics together you will know even more than you did before and that's what's really important, isn't it? I know how hard you work and this means you are improving all the time, even though sometimes games are lost."

'**Even though**' creates more importance or shifts focus to the first part of the sentence.

'**And**' creates' the same importance or gives equal focus to both parts of the sentence it connects.

'**But**' creates more importance or shifts the focus to the second part of the sentence.

Using the words 'even though' has a different effect than 'and' and 'but' in language patterns.

****

Activity:

Have a go at changing some sentences to create a positive focus.

For example: In the following sentence the player begins to speak positively, but changes the focus to make the message negative.

"I won the match, but I didn't get the points I wanted."

Notice that the change of structure below shifts the focus of the sentence.

"I won the match, even though I didn't get the points I wanted."

Now have a go yourself.

1. Think of a statement in which a positive experience is overlooked by the use of the word 'but'.
2. Delete the word 'but' and insert the words 'even though' and notice how this changes the focus of your attention.

****

When you begin to practice thinking about the words you use, and listening carefully to other people speaking, you will find you become more sensitive to picking up negative language patterns. In fact, you begin the process of protecting yourself from the implied negative effects of poor communicators. At the same time, you will begin to use your own words in a conscious way, to influence yourself and those you interact with.

As a sports coach, understanding your athletes and getting inside their heads to understand how they think could be a useful tool. So as we continue learning more about influencing language, let's begin to include how our athletes' language affects them. When I say "Our athletes' language", this is not only the words they are using out loud, it also includes the words they use in their internal dialogue!

"Language shapes the way we think, and determines what we can think about."

Benjamin Lee Whorf

11

THE LANGUAGE OF

A BEGINNER!

*"Language is the armoury of the human mind,
and at once contains the trophies of its past and
the weapons of its future conquests"*

Samuel Taylor Coleridge

In the training environment, I set up a 'tricky task' for the candidate coaches to undertake, and generally, they are unable to perform the task straight away. As they fumble, and mumble, I ask them to describe what they 'were' or how they felt at this point and the descriptions range from 'idiot', 'imbecile', 'stupid', 'incompetent', 'uncoordinated', to very naughty swear words; all of which are captured and recorded onto a flipchart sheet.

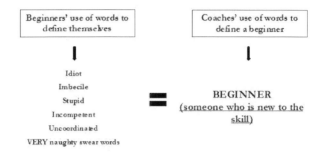

Do you notice how the internal representations of your 'beginners' do not match up with your representation at all? This mismatch of language and thinking is one way you can lose new players in clubs and coaching sessions!

At the cognitive stage of learning there is so much work for the unconscious mind to deal with! There are also negative beliefs, confidence issues, and self-esteem concerns to consider. The coach must understand that these thoughts and beliefs are often lurking in the quiet depths of some beginners' minds. Gently changing these thoughts into positive statements should be uppermost in the coach's mind! So tell me, how do you go about this?

****

Activity:

Experimenting with the effects of language

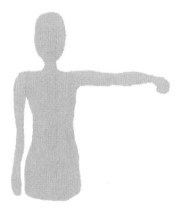

This is a fun exercise that you can do with a friend, which demonstrates the effect that your language (either internal dialogue or external talk) has on your body.

Ask your friend to extend their arm straight out to one side – at shoulder level.

Ask them to repeat out loud "I can, I can, I can, I can, etc". Make sure they keep repeating the phrase out loud.

Tell them to resist as you press down on their arm. You will find it has strong resistance.

Now ask them to repeat "I can't, I can't, I can't, I can't, etc". While they are saying the phrase, press down again on their arm as before. You will find the resistance is weak.

This might be fun, but what does it mean?

Whatever we say to ourselves has a massive effect on our body – every thought we have bathes every cell in our body with either positive or negative energy.

Do you spend your whole day bathing yourself in good positive thoughts or negative ones?

Any internal dialogue should be positive, and focussed on what you want. Never focus on what you don't want!

****

The words you use to your athletes have a direct result on their performance in both their training and their long-term competition results! By ensuring you use power words you will affect their unconscious thinking towards positive results.

POWER WORDS	FAILURE WORDS
Do	Hard
Will	Possibly
Can	Attempt
Able	Not Sure
Easy	Try

These are just a few examples of power and failure words but to keep things simple, a power word is a word that is completely disassociated with any failure and a failure word is one that suggests the possibility of failure.

****

Activity:

Killing the word 'Can't' for a group

Choose a willing volunteer who you judge to have confidence and self-esteem, and who is able to perform press-ups and invite him to the front of the group. Make sure he is fully fit and willing to 'play your game', and also make it clear that this is an experiment that can be fun! All he has to do is follow your instructions fully. Ask him to lie on the floor upon his 'six-pack' (tummy). When you give the command to begin, he is to do the very best press-ups he can, as fast as he can, until he can't do any more and at that point he is free to stop.

Give the signal to start and encourage him; the group may also enjoy giving encouragement too.

When the press-ups come to an end, immediately command the volunteer to do 2/3 more. You might judge that he could do another 1 after that too!

You can then congratulate your volunteer and possibly give out a prize as a thank you. Turn now to your group and state that '.....name of volunteer........'has publicly killed and eliminated the word 'Can't'. The group has no choice except to agree because they witnessed it. As the word has been destroyed, it can be agreed by the group that it may no longer exist in any training sessions. If anyone inadvertently proceeds to bring it back to life, then they themselves must kill it by the use of press-ups.

****

A technique for getting rid of 'Can't' for an individual.

If your athletes are saying 'can't' with their internal dialogue or external talk, how will their success be affected; will they be empowering or disempowering themselves? What can coaches do about this? Be alert to the language you hear your players use.

If a player consistently uses 'Can't', the action I recommend is to first agree with them! This is crucial, because it is true to them. By agreeing with them first, you are pacing them, and opening up any blocks they may have to listening to you. You are also breaking them out of their auto-pilot response. Now you are able to ask the player "Exactly what is stopping you?" Listen to the reply, and then use more investigative questioning and you will be able to eliminate all the blockages until eventually the player is worn down with thinking of excuses, or the matter is dealt with!

An example of this technique

In coaching badminton, a player said he couldn't play a clear. (A forehand stroke played from the rear court to the opposite rear court). I took the player through a step by step process of starting right at the easiest stages:

Me – "I agree that you say you can't play a clear right now. What specifically is stopping you play a clear?"

Player – "I just can't do it at all!"

Me – "Ok, let's have a go at a few things then. Can you hold the racket like this?" (with demonstration)

Player – "Yes of course I can."

Me – "Show me." (See's the player copy correctly) "that's great. Now can you stand like this?" (with demonstration)

Player – "Yes I can." (Copies coach)

Me – "You are doing that just right, well done. Can you move your racket arm like this?" (with demonstration)

Player – "Yes I can"

And so the questioning and copying and praising continued on, one step at a time, with the player agreeing each step and building confidence all the time.

Please note that the player's opinion that they couldn't do a clear was agreed with, and met with only positive statements, and reinforcement of good technique. Eventually the player was practicing on court in a positive manner. The player was encouraged to repeat the words "I can" repeatedly which effects the unconscious mind. Any message we keep repeating is accepted by the unconscious mind as a truth!

Below is an example of how messages heard by others, accepted and repeated by ourselves affect our life.

I woke up one morning at 3.00am with tears streaming into my pillow.

It was during an intensive training weekend, and I was a delegate learning new skills and working on my own personal development. I had wanted to do this passionately, and knew it was going to affect me deeply because of the nature of the course. It was probably one of the biggest keys to unleashing my potential on my pathway of learning and personal growth.

Of course I had been learning lots of this 'stuff' in the years since this journey began. I had been teaching it, applying it, and now at 3.00am on a Sunday morning, alone in a hotel room I had finally absorbed it into my being. My unconscious and conscious came together during my sleep and I finally accepted new and real truths. Some of my old negative and disempowering beliefs were triumphantly and magically shattered into tiny shards of nothingness. The soft silent weeping was due to the enormity of acceptance and the physical relief as the shards of pain were washed away by my tears.

It was here that the true realisation hit me, of how we are truly hypnotised, even by those who love us, sometimes in so many painful ways. And how I, in my ignorance had accepted the words spoken to me. I lay with my head on a damp pillow as I looked back down the years, and remembered clearly the language I was accustomed to hearing, and knew now how this had affected me through 48 years of my life. The feeling of lightness was awesome because the load had slipped away, and I knew that I could simply leave the baggage filled with the lies of my life behind me in that room. In fact I am grateful that I have experienced first-hand the power of releasing old hallucinations and trances, because I can appreciate and empathise with my own clients, as they too press the 'refresh' button, drop their baggage, see their own light, and begin their journeys of discovering who they truly are!

Every one of us is hypnotised, and every one of us hypnotises those around us! I would encourage those who have authority over young people to speak and act according to the best interest of those in their care!

Young children are more susceptible to influence due to their brain wave patterns. Up to the age of seven, their minds are like sponges and are extremely sensitive to all input. They are unable to differentiate facts from fiction, and truth from untruth.

A man ceases to be a beginner in any given science and becomes a master in that science when he has learned that he is going to be a beginner all his life."

Robin G. Collingwood

"Any thought that is passed on to the subconscious often enough and convincingly enough is finally accepted."

Robert Collier

12

USING

IMPECCABLE

LANGUAGE

"It takes tremendous discipline to control the influence, the power you have over other people's lives."

Clint Eastwood

Words are powerful! Our words can, and do make a difference to those who hear them. This has been proven many times by scientific research and within various therapies. This Chapter looks at impeccable language. Impeccable language in this instance means that it is clean and builds confidence, trust and self-esteem for the receiver.

In Don Miguel's book The Four Agreements, we are treated to words of wisdom regarding the power of our words. He explores how we each view the world based on our beliefs and how these are passed on to us through society, our parents, and most importantly, through the spoken word. We are advised by Don to be impeccable with our words, and I completely agree with his teachings. How many coaches have I seen and heard using sarcasm, not only to adults but also to young children.

I come across sarcasm daily. It is used unwittingly by those who have accepted it as part of their communication style. If they are questioned about it their response is usually defensive. "Oh I don't mean any harm", "I was only kidding", "They shouldn't be so sensitive/silly". These sorts of statements are often made in defence of using sarcasm. So does this mean then that the listener should be responsible and ignore cutting remarks and comments that put one down, etc? Should we all grow such a thick skin that we don't feel pain and therefore we can inflict pain on another without thinking?

Sarcasm is the use of words to damage the reputation of, or hurt, another person. It is a sharp, bitter, or cutting expression or remark; a bitter jibe or taunt.

Interpretation is different to each listener; some people and especially children take things very personally. Have you ever worked with people with special needs and noticed how many take your words literally? Very young children also take things literally. Unfortunately, children who are exposed to sarcasm frequently grow thick skins to protect themselves from the lies and hurts of the speaker. Very often these are their parents, and of course children model themselves on their parents, so quickly they too use sarcasm as a part of their own communication system. The use of sarcasm can also be described as a form of bullying since its intention is to hurt or degrade another person.

If I were to pay you a compliment, would you think I was being sarcastic (funny), or would you believe me?

Many people find it hard to receive genuine praise because of their own use of sarcasm, or because they have grown such a thick skin that they cannot accept praise, probably because they can no longer tell the difference!

So what can we do?

Firstly we need to clean up our own language! When we speak, we must be careful with our use of words. We must speak with integrity, and use our words to build and encourage others and remove all need to gossip or use sarcasm!

We can stop taking things personally. Remember, whatever other people say is a projection of themselves and of their own reality. When we are immune to the opinions and talk of others, we release needless suffering!

We can stop making assumptions and ask questions instead. It takes time and courage to ask what people are really saying, so that we can be sure we understand the meaning of what is being said. We can take responsibility for ensuring we are truly understood by others by using clear communication skills ourselves.

That leaves us with choices doesn't it? We can choose to step up and take responsibility for our communication. This means we can hurt and bully, or be thoughtful and empowering. We can choose to ignore comments from those who use the bullying of sarcasm through their own lack of knowledge and confidence, because we know it says more about them than about us.

Oh, and by the way, who do you think is responsible for good communication – the listener or the speaker? Are you able to accept the responsibility of excellence in communication?

****

Activity:

This is an exercise to help you make changes in your own language patterns. When you have carried out the activity you may begin to notice remarkable changes around you.

For a period of seven days, only say what you mean, get rid of all sarcasm!

If you make a mistake and use sarcasm, then restart your seven days, even if it occurred on the seventh day!

Now, depending on how often and how long you have used sarcasm, it may only take seven days to create a new habit, or it may take considerably longer.

However, by simply beginning again, and patiently persisting with the activity you will definitely remove this old negative style of bullying language patterns, and install empowering language. This means that you are a leader who is inspirational and helps to build confidence and self-worth in others.

****

Remember:

As a coach you are in a position of authority and powerful influence. The words you use and the way you speak to your athletes have lasting consequences on each individual. Your influence on your athletes is not limited to their sport, but to their wider, everyday experiences of living and interacting in society!

Inspire people!

Never use Sarcasm

Speak with integrity

Praise sincerely

Intend a positive outcome

Respect everyone

Enjoy your results

"The true teacher defends his pupils against his own personal influence. He inspires self-distrust. He guides their eyes from himself to the spirit that quickens him. He will have no disciple."

Amos Bronson Alcott

"Nothing is more discouraging than unappreciated sarcasm."

unknown source

"Sarcasm I now see to be, in general, the language of the devil; for which reason I have long since as good as renounced it."

Thomas Carlyle

13

BOOSTING

PERFORMANCE

"All growth depends upon activity. There is no development physically or intellectually without effort, and effort means work."

Calvin Coolidge

Whilst coaching, I wonder how many children you have noticed who find it difficult to accept praise? In fact, if you think about it, how good are you at accepting praise? I have worked with a fellow coach who gave me the strangest look simply because I said "Thank-you" to him! What meaning do you give to that? Apparently during a lifetime of working in a setting where sarcasm was prevalent and was the normal communication style, he now thinks that praise is untrue, insincere and sarcastic. I suppose that, just as I cannot understand sarcasm and accept the words said by another as real, other people may not believe in my sincerity when I give praise and thanks either!! Can you notice that chasm of misunderstandings!

But let's get back to the children we coach, and remember how many find it difficult to accept praise. It is hardly surprising that children find receiving praise difficult. After all, many of us have become accustomed to looking for negatives. As coaches, we are trained to look for faults and problems to correct; teachers are continuously pointing out weaknesses and then, "Oh dear", we come to the main child-programmers, the parents themselves! Research carried out in California counted positive and negative statements by parents to children that recorded, on average, that for every 35 positive statements there were around 372 negative ones! Are you aware that to delete one negative statement it can take 10 positive ones?

Self-image is a blue print for a person's life. It is this blue-print that determines the results we each get. So what is self image? You can't see it or touch it; nevertheless it is as real as the person who owns it. It forms the reality of your world; it is the inner picture of yourself, which is your own opinion of yourself!

We are shaped by our thoughts; we become what we think.

Self-image is constructed and maintained through our thoughts (inner dialogue), and external language patterns. That voice you hear constantly inside your head is either your best friend or your biggest foe! I'm hoping that some people wouldn't speak to a stranger the way they speak to themselves!

I came to realise that often in the past, the voice I heard told me some really ugly lies that I believed in completely, and my actions confirmed these as did my results!

Going through my teenage years thinking that I was completely unattractive and not very clever, meant that I had little aspiration, and no big dreams!

I was scared to speak openly or share any small opinions I had at the time. Even if anyone said that I looked attractive, I thought that they were being sarcastic and I certainly didn't believe them! From where I am now, seeing my daughter grow through her teenage years, blossoming and looking terrific, I realise that this is how I looked way back then. The similarities between our looks at that age are striking; so how could I then have thought I was so ugly?

I don't think it's any good arguing with a person about their self-image, because an embedded belief is like a prolific weed in the garden. You can pull up the leaves but unless you remove the root completely it grows back as vigorously as ever! Psychologists have techniques to loosen and to finally change beliefs; sports coaches who apply positive coaching techniques and some simple NLP patterns can also begin to loosen some beliefs in their athletes. The younger an athlete is, the easier it is to begin to make changes.

Self-image has a major impact on behaviour and responses to any situation. For example, if a beginner to sport has the belief that they are a 'loser', then they will be very challenged to participate in anything that is competitive and, if they do, they simply expect to lose. This means they have negative body language which boosts the confidence of the opposition, making them even more dominant.

Research has shown that we use the reactions of others to ourselves, as a confirmation that our own beliefs are true! This leads to a self fulfilling prophesy.

Coaches who are able to assist change in the way athletes perceive themselves can have a direct effect on behaviour.

"Relentless, repetitive self talk is what changes our self-image."

Denis Waitley

"The person we believe ourselves to be will always act in a manner consistent with our self-image."

Brian Tracy

14

USING THE RETICULAR ACTIVATOR TO MAKE CHANGES

"If you think you can do a thing or think you can't do a thing, you're right."

Henry Ford

Change the Belief, and the Result Changes

Most people live their whole lives never knowing they have a personal Reticular Activator System (RAS) hidden away and working hard to ensure you get what you think about!

This 'genie' within, lies at the base of the brain and is on alert 24 hours a day, seven days a week! Its prime function is to make us notice things that are either threatening, or unusual, or familiar or important to us. Right now, at this moment you have around you 2 million different bits of sensory information every second. Your brain can only cope with around 135 bits a second, so your RAS has the job of sorting out which bits are important to you at any one time. The RAS acts as a filter in our brain, filtering out unnecessary information. Stop reading for a few seconds and notice all the sounds around you. Notice the sensations that you can you feel? You may become more aware of your breathing, blinking and any smells, or the air temperature and air movement around you. The RAS filtered out all these sensations whilst you were reading. The RAS focuses directly on what is important to each of us and filters out the rest.

The Reticular Activator System

The RAS has a wide variety of functions such as walking, elimination, sex and eating. It's most important function is to control consciousness, wakefulness, and sleep. The RAS is an amazing filter system that is programmed by the beliefs we have installed. Imagine that you have your own personal gatekeeper, this gatekeeper works on your behalf doing everything you have programmed it to do with absolutely no questioning! This gatekeeper has access to your every belief and actively looks for everything that reinforces your belief, ensuring that absolutely nothing else gets in! For instance, if you believe the world is full of angry men (because maybe your father was mostly angry), then that's exactly what you will be allowed to notice!

Understanding that beliefs are installed by perceptions of events, memories, people and language during the formative years, means that you can begin to appreciate the depth and strength of beliefs, and how a person can have such strong beliefs, even in something that is totally false!

Below is an example of how some beliefs can affect results.

NOTE: A belief can be anything you buy into and choose to believe, it does not have to be true!

How many beliefs did you once believe were true, and now believe are no longer true? Santa Claus, tooth fairies, eating crusts makes your hair curl, girls/boys are horrible, 21 is old! Stepping under a ladder is unlucky! Think back through history. How many beliefs have been disproved with more knowledge! 'The earth is flat'; 'Man will never fly!'

How many wars have been fought over differences of beliefs?

What beliefs do you have that are empowering or disempowering you, and how many of them are really true?

What beliefs do your athletes carry with them that prevent them from getting the results they want?

Every word we use works on the RAS. Whatever you think about is what you get. A great deal of research has been done on the subject and is readily available to read on the internet and in books.

There are coaches who advise players in the following ways - "Don't hit it to HIM," "Don't hit it OUT!" "Don't miss the shot," -I am sure you will know by now that this actually focuses the athlete on what not to do! The golfer who is told "Don't hit into those bunkers" suddenly realises there are bunkers he hadn't even noticed before, and they are now foremost in his mind!

The sooner you begin to **SAY WHAT YOU WANT** the sooner you get excellent results. So, say what you want, what you really, really want! Only say what you actually want your player to do, because this goes into the RAS which focuses on doing EXACTLY that! Some coaches like to tell, and even show their athletes what they are doing wrong, before they tell them the corrections. When the athlete leaves the session, or plays the sport later on, the conflicting right and wrong ways of doing the technique can become cloudy, and produce uncertainty. Or the player may only remember the incorrect method! When you give only positive instructions to your athlete you create faster learning, because the messages don't get mixed up with what not to do.

Train your players to focus on what they want to achieve too, because if they focus on not losing and not making a mistake, that is what will happen!

Encourage your athletes to pay attention to their inner voice. What is their self-talk saying? If they are repeating negatives such as "I can't do it", or "Don't make a mistake", etc, help them to notice it quickly, and change the thought into a new positive one.

Remember:

• You can only hold one thought at a time; make sure it is a helpful one

• Your RAS filters all information and allows in only that which confirms whatever you are focussing on

• You can train your RAS with affirmations and visualisation techniques

• You can influence your athletes' RAS by the way you communicate; by the words you choose to use.

"You see things, and you say why? But I dream things that never were, and I say why not?"

George Bernard Shaw

"You can have anything you want if you give up the belief that you can't have it."

Dr. Robert Anthony

"The outer conditions of a person's life will always be found to reflect their inner beliefs."

James Allen

"If you believe you can, you probably can. If you believe you won't, you most assuredly won't. Belief is the ignition switch that gets you off the launching pad."

Denis Waitley

15

SELF SABOTAGE!

"Latent in every man is a venom of amazing bitterness, a black resentment; something that curses and loathes life, a feeling of being trapped, of having trusted and been fooled, of being the helpless prey of impotent rage, blind surrender, the victim of a savage, ruthless power that gives and takes away, enlists a man, and crowning injury inflicts upon him the humiliation of feeling sorry for himself."

Paul Valery

Are your athletes sabotaging their own success?

How many times have you heard your athletes make comments such as:

"I never play well on that court!"

"That opponent always makes me lose!"

"I can never hit straight with that 'iron/racket/bat'!"

"I have always hated the lighting in that stadium."

"The bars in that gym always make me feel unbalanced."

Thinking negative thoughts leads to negative emotions which in turn affect your physiology and leads to failure. This is a self-fulfilling prophesy.

Even a top level athlete who is technically and tactically competent, who is strong, fit and healthy, can succumb from a lack of self-belief and poor self-talk. It causes low confidence and low self-image. In order to help build confidence with affirmations, it is important for an athlete to have a genuine belief in himself, and for the coach to identify where and when the athlete's self-belief starts to break down.

When people fail to do something once or more, they can quickly become helpless. There is some correlation here between those who have optimistic tendencies and those who lean towards pessimism! The following activity quickly demonstrates learned helplessness.

****

Activity:

This activity is for you to experiment with the concept of learned helplessness. All you need is 2 to 4 friends some paper and pens.

Prepare 2 different anagram tests by writing the following tests onto separate sheets of paper.

Test one:- 1) BAT 2) LEMON 3) LNOODN.

Test two – 1) WHIRL 2) SLAPSTICK 3) LNOODN.

Make sure your friends don't know there are 2 different tests as you hand these out FACE DOWN! with pens. (Use more test 1's than 2's).

NOTE: Test 2 questions 1 and 2 are unsolvable because they are not anagrams.

Introduce the activity as simple anagrams to be solved one at a time. You indicate when to start with number one. They are to put up their hand when they have completed. When hands start to go up, move them on to the next question etc.

Test 1 is very easy to solve and hands will go up quickly; the answers are TAB, MELON, LONDON. Test 2 anagrams 1 and 2 are impossible to solve, but number 3 is the same for both tests and is just a little harder than the first 2 questions in test 1.

Even though anagram 3 is identical in both tests you will discover that most people doing test 2 will be unable to solve it!

****

Dealing with learned helplessness as a coach

When a child fails in sport for whatever reason, it is important that the child knows and appreciates that they can take responsibility on how to deal with it. If they are beaten by an older more experienced player, they need to understand the reason. They can then make a decision to keep training so that they too can become stronger.

When new athletes come to your sessions for the first time, they may be carrying all sorts of negative thinking with them about their performance, Their belief that they are failures already will greatly impact on their efforts to train and improve. In fact, they will be looking for more failures to confirm their poor beliefs! Think how this will be reinforced in an atmosphere of sarcasm, ridicule, teasing from other players, or even volunteers/coaches? When we see a child seeming not to try, or fooling about, maybe we can be more open in the meanings we give to this behaviour.

Sports psychologists suggest that athletes need a basic confidence and early images of success. The experts share the opinion that in some cases there is a need for athletes to explore traumas, humiliations, past failures, and embarrassments from their childhoods past unconscious memories.

A memory of having a negative experience in a specific situation can trigger a repetition of a similar negative experience. Take for instance, a tournament player who loses an important match in a specific venue which creates a significant emotional impact. The player can have that memory triggered at a crucial point when they return to that same venue. A trigger causes an athlete to reflect on their past performance, and creates an expectation of a similar experience.

We can reverse this process by helping our athletes to develop their own self-belief of success. If they can develop their own set of positive statements about themselves and their performance, they will begin to change their old negative self-beliefs and self-talk. Such positive statements are known as Affirmations. Affirmations can be used to create strong empowering mindsets for ourselves and for our athletes.

Do you remember the Boxing legend, Muhammad Ali? If so, I am sure you remember the following:

Before a bout, wrapped in his boxing robe, dancing from side to side, he would proclaim; "Float like a butterfly, sting like a bee."

At the end of a match, He yells, "I'm the king of the world, I am the greatest, I'm Muhammad Ali. I shook up the world, I am the greatest, I'm king of the world. I'm pretty, I'm pretty, I'm a baaaad man, you heard me, I'm a baaad man."

Muhammad Ali had harnessed the power of positive thinking, creating his own personal affirmations which he repeated so often, that people can still remember them long after he finished his last fight many years ago!

And what about Ali's results? From 1960 to 1963, the young fighter amassed a record of 19-0 with 15 knock-outs!

Remember:

- Learned helplessness has a negative impact

- Make certain you create practices that challenge and stretch your players' abilities, yet at the same time your players still find them manageable

- Find out what beliefs your athletes have that are going to limit their success, and help them to create new more empowering beliefs.

"A strong, positive self-image is the best possible preparation for success."

Joyce Brothers

"Success is not final, failure is not fatal: it is the courage to continue that counts."

Winston Churchill

16

CREATING POSITIVE AFFIRMATIONS FOR SPORT

"Practice rather than preach. Make of your life an affirmation, defined by your ideals, not the negation of others. Dare to the level of your capability then go beyond to a higher level."

Alexander King

Performance is 90% Perception and 10% Reality

An Affirmation is simply an emotionally charged statement that can create positive beliefs and behaviours.

Before we go on to helping our athletes create their affirmations, what about you the coach? What affirmations are you using for yourself? After all, why should a player learn from you if you are not following your own advice?

If you have followed the earlier chapters, you may already have experienced the power of using positive statements. Perhaps you have turned around your negative beliefs by creating new words. However, now we are going to harness the power of affirmations, we are going to introduce these to our athletes and teach them the benefits of doing affirmations that influence deep changes.

Always remember that the mind and body are so closely aligned that the mind cannot tell what is real, or dreamed, or imagined. The central nervous system and the body respond to the images that the mind creates.

Affirmations specific to sporting situations are used in many contexts:

- Aid concentration
- Build confidence
- Improve performance
- Help relaxation and well being
- Help speed up recovery from injury
- Reduce fear and negativity
- Improve strength and endurance
- I'm sure you will be able to think of many more.

How to do Affirmations

Write down your affirmations! Writing is powerful and, just as in goal setting, seeing your affirmations in written form has a positive benefit to your mind.

There are many ways to write down your affirmations and here are a few suggestions:

- Use a beautiful journal to record your affirmations

- Write them at least 9 times

- Write them (and say them) in the first, second and third person. When you decided to create a negative belief you may have experienced someone saying "you are stupid" or overheard people saying "Freddy is stupid", and then you reinforced it by repeating "I am stupid". So affirmations in this example could be: "You are able to do many things". "Freddy (insert your own name) is able to do many things". "I am able to do many things"

- Write your affirmation twice; once using your dominant hand AND again using your non-dominant hand. This accesses both sides of the brain.

The Rules for Successful Affirmations

Make them positive: The unconscious mind is literal; if you say "I must not tighten my muscles", the mind only focuses on the word 'tighten'. Instead, say "I allow my muscles to relax easily".

State them in the present: Act as if it is happening NOW! When the affirmation is stated in the future tense the mind will always work to the future and it will never be in the present!

Use self-image statements: They can be stated as I can, I allow, I am, I know.

Keep them short: They are easier to remember this way.

Be authentic: This means your affirmation is for you and is based exactly on what you want be, do, or have.

Be specific: State exactly what it is you want to be, do, or have.

Energise your Affirmations!: Repeat your affirmations using a positive voice tone, speak with the appropriate energy, stand tall, shoulders back, smile as you say them and visualise yourself actualising the words as you say them! This is a VITAL step for succeeding with your affirmations!

Dealing with conflict when using Affirmations

Until you have practiced and realised the effectiveness and good results of using affirmations, you may be sceptical and wonder how on earth you can believe a lie!

Below are a few ideas to ensure that you reconcile any conflicts:

Word the affirmation in such a way that you can believe it! For instance if you lack confidence in matches, an affirmation could be "I have the seeds of confidence within me right now" or "Every time I play my sport my confidence grows stronger"

Turn your affirmation into a question. For example, instead of saying "I am confident" say instead "What can I do to gain confidence?" The words 'gain' and 'confidence' are still going into your unconscious mind and your RAS is being programmed to look for ways of building confidence.

Acknowledge that an affirmation is not exactly a fact, but a stepping stone on your way to achieving what you actually want.

Use two sheets of paper. On the first sheet write your affirmation. On the second sheet, record the reactions you feel when you read it. For instance, sheet 1 – "I am confident" - sheet 2 "You must be joking". Continue this process – the same affirmation 20+ times and immediately recording your first thoughts until you notice that your thinking is aligning positively to the affirmation you have written!

Activating Affirmations

Practice ways to strengthen your affirmations. For the affirmation "Every time I play my sport my confidence grows stronger", go on court ensuring your physiology is that of a confident person. This means you will be standing and walking erect, you will engage your centre (see previous chapters), your head will be level, and your voice will be heard when you speak.

Remember that your physiology and mental state is so closely linked that working on one affects the other.

Using Affirmations

The first step is writing down the affirmation, and we have already looked at that, heard the message and experienced doing the task. Now, to strengthen the results, be creative! Write down your affirmations on sticky-notes or on card, laminate them, decorate them, draw or use pictures with them that illustrate your intentions, and put them in places where you will see them. You could choose to stick them on a bathroom mirror, in a wallet or purse, on a car dashboard, in a sports bag, stuck inside trainers, in your diary, make a book mark and use it as a screen saver on your computer...................... The important point of this is that you constantly notice your affirmations and they are being reinforced into your unconscious mind by repetition!

When preparing for competition use the previous methods to create affirmations to help you prepare mentally. Leave them in places that you will notice at different points of the day leading up to and during, your competition.

Be Creative!

Create your personal slide show with inspirational music and photos of you, and images of the success or goals you want to achieve.

Make a recording of your affirmations that lasts for at least 10 minutes, using the format mentioned above; e.g,

- I Freddy, am growing in confidence daily
- You are more confident today
- Freddy, you are gaining confidence every day
- I am enjoying noticing new confidence growing within me.

Use a background of 'brain-music' to your affirmations, because it enhances the programming process, especially if you listen to this just before you sleep! Play the recording at any time of the day and you won't even need to consciously listen to it, because your unconscious mind notices EVERYTHING!!

Have Fun!

Think back to Muhammad Ali and his wide variety of affirmations! Have a look and listen to him as he says them – he has lots on U Tube! Notice the way he says them, the energy in his voice AND his physiology! See his expressions, hear his vocal tones, feel his power!

What affirmations can you have for yourself as a coach? What message would you wish to convey?

And what about setting your athletes a task of designing affirmations that they could use to motivate themselves and maybe just maybe, affect the opposition

****

Activity:

Here's my one of my own affirmations

"I don't just coach, I inspire. My players are winners, they perform, they're on fire!

Now have some fun with thinking up your own 'Muhammad Ali' style affirmations, either as a sports participant or a coach!

………………………………………………………

………………………………………………………

………………………………………………………

………………………………………………………

………………………………………………………

………………………………………………………

How did you get on? The more you practice – the easier it is and if you're going to get your athletes to do affirmations. I'm sure you want to lead by example.

****

It was very interesting for me to do my own personal affirmations. The one above felt very strange indeed when I first wrote it! In the beginning I didn't even like to look at it, as I felt rather embarrassed. However, as I kept returning to it and saying it out loud, I found myself slowly becoming more comfortable, then at ease, and finally, finding myself thoroughly believing it. Now I find it fascinating that the word 'Inspiration' is a part of my own website! I have received many testimonials that say I have inspired someone! I have quite a few personal affirmations which I use, and am constantly finding how affective they are proving to be.

I am sure you will find using affirmations works for you, and that your athletes also discover the power in creating personal affirmations.

"As a single footstep will not make a path on the earth, so a single thought will not make a pathway in the mind. To make a deep physical path, we walk again and again. To make a deep mental path, we must think over and over the kind of thoughts we wish to dominate our lives."

Henry David Thoreau,

Author, Poet, and Philosopher

17

VISUALISATION

"I've discovered that numerous peak performers use the skill of mental rehearsal of visualization. They mentally run through important events before they happen."

Charles A. Garfield

At the University of Chicago, a basketball team was selected to test their free throwing skills, and were split into three groups for the experiment.

The first group practiced their skills for one hour every day for 30 days.

The second group were allowed to sit in the gym but were not to touch the balls, and to only visualise themselves throwing the balls through the hoops.

The third group was the control group and neither physically practiced nor mentally rehearsed their skills.

On the 31st day the players were assessed on their throwing skills. The control group went first to set the bench-mark. The first group who had practiced for 30 days scored 24% more hoops than the control group. I don't suppose this surprises you does it?

However the visualising group scored 23% more hoops than the control group, which was only 1% below those who had physically practiced. Yet they hadn't touched the ball for 30 days!

Summarising this research, it is clear that simply visualising an outcome has incredible power within it. Imagine the power of putting visualisation and physical practice together!

What is Visualisation?

Visualisation is also called mental imagery, mental rehearsal, autogenic training or even self hypnosis. It is a process used both in sport and in business for creating an intention or mental image, for any result or goal you want to achieve.

In "The Script Journal" Ryan Williams writes that;

"Good screenwriters know that fear generates a core emotional response that actually changes the body's chemical response for a small period in time. This shift inside an audience, in turn, creates thrilling moments in which their participation actually engages them physically with the stories on the screen. This is because horror films are emotion-based experiences."

How it Works

The brain cannot differentiate between reality and imagination. Every time we think, the hypothalamus within the brain releases chemicals that correspond directly to each thought. You can check it out for yourself, when you watch a scary movie, or perhaps are truly scared, there are certain changes you may notice; muscles tighten, your heart rate increase and maybe you feel cold, or your hairs stand up on the back of your neck.

The brain is divided into two hemispheres; the left side is the logical, analytical, rational thinking side, and the right side is the creative, intuitive, imaginative side which is totally accepting, and therefore acts towards your desires with no judgement.

Who can Visualise?

If you watch children play you will notice how often they use imagination naturally and easily. A cardboard box becomes a car, a den, a table;

imaginary friends and pets are common. When dressing up, little girls become princesses, boys become soldiers and events can seem very real.

When using visualisation with a group of small children in a generic sports group that I ran, I can remember vividly when one tiny tot cried real tears of fear when it was her turn to 'walk the plank' in a game of 'Pirates'! We had to stop the game and explain that it was 'just pretend' until she calmed down.

When you read novels, what do you notice? Are you aware of black markings on white paper or do you see images in your mind's eye? Do you hear the sounds, feel emotions, and maybe salivate and imagine smells and tastes? Probably, most of us do much of this when we are reading our favourite novel, and some of you may be similar to me, imagining the events as real whilst you are so engrossed. This is using your imagination, or visualising.

You may be among the majority of people who find it easy and natural to visualise, whereas some find it easier to hear or feel things. Whichever way you begin to visualise with intention doesn't matter, it becomes easier with practice. Once you are skilled, it is even easy to visualise with your eyes open.

How to Visualise

Visualisation is easy, natural, and can be done anywhere at any time, although it is not recommended to do this whilst driving, or when needing to concentrate on a job in hand!

Just close your eyes right now and think of a time when you were on holiday or really enjoying yourself somewhere

....

Chances are that you found yourself smiling, and that you experienced a feeling of well-being that may even linger on. This sense of feeling good is due to the release of endorphins, nature's own natural narcotic which causes you to feel happy. Remember though, in order to do this, the visualisation or memory should be a positive one.

An excellent time to visualise is when you are in bed just before you go to sleep. Whilst you are drifting down into theta brain waves, visualisation is extremely effective because this is when your subconscious mind is most easily influenced.

Three steps of Visualisation

Step 1

To visualise, you can either sit or lie down and simply fire up your imagination. Use some music, relaxation, or meditation techniques to relax your body and mind. If you are guiding an individual or group you can, if you need to, read from a relaxation script.

Step 2

Begin to imagine your goal or intention and make it in the present. When you create an image make sure you are looking through your own eyes. Imagine the sounds around you in this situation, and where they are coming from. Notice any emotions you are having, and the feelings within you and around you. If you are holding something, what does it feel like, what is the temperature of the object, and what is the temperature around you? Are you hot or cold? If it is a cold place, you might notice vapour as you exhale. If you are hot then what does feel like when you sweat? Are there any smells that you might be aware of, or tastes? Visualise the look and feel of your clothing and equipment; your posture; the surroundings in detail; and if other people are involved, their details. Give everything as much detail as you can.

Step 3

Practice visualising daily - twice a day if possible.

Examples of using visualisation within sport

An example of visualisation I use with my players, I lead them through a guided visualisation to mentally rehearse, imagining what it could possibly feel like to be one of the world's top performers at the sport. My badminton group will stand in a ready position in the centre of a badminton court with their eyes closed and be led through a guided visualisation, which allows the player to create visual images, the sounds, feelings/ sensations/ emotions, smells (and tastes if appropriate) of moving around the court prior to an international performance. Questions and instructions such as "What would it feel like?" "Notice how fast/ smoothly/ elegantly/ effortlessly you are able to move". "Become aware of the feel of your racket/ the control/ power/accuracy as you use it to open up the court/move the opposition/win the rally". "Notice the sounds of the racket as you make your strokes, the sound of the shuttle being struck, see the shuttle fly fast or slow – exactly as you choose every time you hit it".

These examples would be a very short visualisation exercise followed by a shadowing activity with the racket, moving around and playing strokes as if in a game of singles. I would be re-emphasising the positive components of the visualisation as the players perform the shadowing exercise.

Although some players may be bemused, or find it strange to begin with, the feedback I have received is that performance during the session following this activity is higher, and players have mentioned they had played better than they had ever done previously.

During a training session you can use visualisation to accelerate learning, for example in a net shot for badminton where the technique is to have the racket head below the racket hand so that it is angled downwards when it strikes the shuttle. I often ask the players to 'see a mountain' just in front of the net. They describe the colour of their mountain, what is on the mountain whilst looking at the place in front of the net where the mountain is sited. At the same time I am pointing to the mountain, outlining its whereabouts and looking intently at it as I question them, and agree that it is a very fine mountain indeed! The shuttle needs to be struck on the other side of that mountain and the racket therefore needs to go OVER the mountain and return the same way! This gives the racket a good technical pathway to follow, and the resulting accurate techniques are immediate and long lasting, which means that the visualisation is extremely effective.

At the end of a training session visualisation during stretches can enhance the benefits of the stretching by relaxing the mind, reinforcing positive points of the performance and increasing flexibility. Athletes can visualise muscles and tendons, the colours, imagining seeing them lengthening, relaxing, growing stronger, becoming more flexible. What else could you add to your warm downs?

Just as we coach and train physical aspects of our sport, we need to apply the same principles to coach and train our athletes to create and use visualisation skills effectively. The four elements (4R's) to remember are Relaxation, Realism, Regularity, and Reinforcement.

If you are working with young children, you will probably find that they enjoy activities that are imaginative and fun. Many governing bodies have special programmes that encourage imaginative games whilst teaching fundamental or basic skills. Badminton England for example has BISI which includes activities based on Snow White, visiting the North Pole, and becoming a frog, amongst a host of others. You may agree that learning is easier and faster if the sessions are fun, and in my experience the more imaginative the session is, particularly for the younger children, the more fun we have.

Aspects of visualising can be used throughout any coaching session from the start and warming up, right through to the stretches at the end. I have taught visualisation to my players and use it in most sessions at some point, and maybe you already do the same.

Visualisation can be used by any athlete of any sport, at any age and by all abilities! Just as athletes practice their physical skills, regularity is essential for training with visualisation. Practice using it during training sessions, pre-competitions, and encourage your athletes to use it at home every day. It can even be performed as you are walking or travelling by public transport, though I wouldn't advise it whilst driving!

Reinforcement

Writing a personal visualisation script can be a useful tool, especially if this is recorded, so that it can be listened to repeatedly before sleep.

Create a personal visualisation board. Collect images of what you want to achieve: medals, pictures of winners; images of success; the body you want to achieve; top athletes you aspire to be like; any image that you find to represent the way you want to feel/look; where you want to be etc. Position the board where it will be a constant reminder.

Use a scrapbook to put in images just the same way as the visualisation board. Paste in your own affirmations and any records of previous successes.

Have fun with your creations and refer to this regularly.

Create your own movie or slide show using downloaded images, photos, music, affirmations, quotes – again anything that will inspire and help you to visualise your goals.

****

Activity:

This is a visualisation exercise you can try out for yourself. You can choose to read the script to someone else or have it read it out to you. You may also be surprised when you notice what is happening even when you read the script.

Close your eyes and take a big breath in.................... and release. As you breath out you can allow your muscles to simply relax and notice your shoulders drop as you do this now hold out one of your hands in front of you palm upwards and just imagine a lemon appearing in this open palm. Imagine becoming aware of its shade of yellow, the shape, you could feel the waxiness of its skin and notice its weight as it lies there in front of you. Now what would it feel like to use two hands to break this lemon in two, the softness as your fingers are squeezed into it, and the coolness as they break through the skin and enter deep into its flesh, the phishing sound as juice squirts out over your hands, and the astringent citrusy aroma is powerful and zesty.

Slowly watch as you bring the lemon towards your mouth, notice the gleam of the open flesh, with its moistness and acidity, and now you can bring its wetness into your mouth feeling the coolness as you bite down into the flesh and skin together.........................

Is your mouth-watering yet? Some of you may also have noticed soreness if you had a cut on your hand when the lemon juice was released!

****

You can see from doing the simple activity above, that visualisation or imagination has a direct effect on a person's physiology. What positive implications do you think this has when using visualisation with your athletes?

"What this power is I cannot say, all I know is that it exists and it becomes available only when a man is in that state of mind in which he knows exactly what he wants and is fully determined not to quit until he finds it."

Alexander Graham Bell

18

SIMPLE STATE CHANGE

"The greatest revolution of our generation is the discovery that human beings, by changing the inner attitudes of their minds, can change the outer aspects of their lives."

William James *(psychologist)*

How to change a 'LOSING' mindset into a 'WINNING' one, in a matter of minutes!

Do any of your players get into such a 'state of nerves' before an important match, so that their performance drops? Do you see some players get themselves worked up into a 'state of anger' over line calls, etc which spoils their focus, concentration and control? How do those negative states compare to a player getting into 'the zone' or into a 'state of alertness, readiness, concentration and/or focus'?

What about you when you are coaching? What 'state' do you choose to do when you are working? Is it one of excitement, concentration and confidence, or maybe uncertainty, or frustration? What would it be like if you could become aware of any negative current states, and could create more useful positive states in yourself and help your players to do the same?

The idea of 'State' or State of Mind' refers to how the processes of mind and body affect a person at any given time.

A state is comprised of the ongoing mental and physical conditions from which a person is acting, and it filters and affects the final results or the interpretation of these results.

The word 'state' can be used to describe your way of 'being' at any given moment. It includes your mood, or present emotion, energy level, the way you hold and use your body, and the way you think. It is a collaboration of many things, with numerous names e.g.: Tired, Happy, Sad, Excited, Enthusiastic, Miserable, Fascinated, Passionate, Loving, Angry etc.

Usually, we don't notice our state unless we are in a very different one from our normal 'baseline' state. We are all constantly changing and using different states as we move through different experiences and contexts in our day to day living, and everyone manages their state to some degree. For example, "I'll go for a nice walk to make me feel better", "I will watch a funny film for a laugh", "I will go out with friends and get drunk". All these are merely strategies to change a current state, but some of them, you may agree, can be harmful in the long term.

As you pass from state to state, you may think of them as good or bad, desirable or not, and you know which ones you enjoy and those you don't!

Have you ever noticed that your whole world changes, or seems to change when your mood or 'state' changes? This means we have a basis for deciding whether to keep, increase, or change a state to another one.

It is possible to learn how to choose our own state, and doing this increases our ability to use flexible behaviours and generates a higher probability of achieving desired outcomes.

Managing your State

In order to manage your state, you need to understand what effects it, and the NLP communications model helps with that. This has already been covered.

Your 'state' is a part of your communication system, and as such reacts to any changes made in other parts of the system.

External Event

Most people think that our state changes because of an external event. How many times do you hear people make comments such as, "He cheated, and made me angry", "She jumped out and made me scared", "He bought me flowers and made me feel loved", "That player looks fierce and makes me nervous".

However, imagine two young badminton players playing in their first tournament and losing by a large margin. One player comes off court and says "That was so exciting, I learnt so much", whilst the other player comes off court crying!

This is an identical event, but the states that are created are completely different! Events then, in and of themselves, are completely neutral and are neither good nor bad! A state is created by way we 'look' at the event through our personal filter system, and by deciding which label to stick on the event! Even when an event is considered 'bad' by a majority of people, the event itself remains neutral and it only means that the group has filtered it in a similar way.

This concept has far reaching implications, and it is well worth taking some time to contemplate this in your own life. It means accepting that you are responsible for your emotions/states, regardless of any event!

States are easy to change when we understand how easily we can change our filtering system! For example a person who has a phobia of dogs thinks that ALL events with dogs are terrifying and therefore responds with a state of terror. However, you probably already know that phobias can be cured. The 'cure' actually involves changing the way the information is filtered so that a dog event is processed differently, creating a different 'state'.

Internal Event

States can also be created by our imagination and our perceived memory.

Even though we are far removed from the imagined event or memory, the mere thought of it can evoke powerful state changes!

The following activity demonstrates the power of the connection of our thoughts to our states.

****

Activity:

Each time you do these exercises, be aware of changes in your posture and breathing. What changes of state do you feel?

- Think back and remember an old argument, how do you feel?

- Think back and remember a wonderful holiday, how do you feel?

- Think forwards to an exciting event somewhere in your future, how do you feel?

Now work with a friend. Ask them the questions above and notice the changes you see in their posture, expressions and breathing. Give them time to access their thoughts/memories.

****

Doing the activity above demonstrates the power of the connection of our thoughts to our states.

The Effect of Behaviour and Posture on States

Behaviour can be defined as any actions we undertake. Compare the effect to your mood (state) of the following activities; a brisk walk on a beautiful day to sitting in a cluttered, airless, windowless office. The former would surely lift your spirits, whereas the latter would change your state to lacklustre.

You are likely to consider slumped over shoulders, dropped head, eyes looking down, slow pace and speech, and poor posture to indicate a person is feeling 'down' or depressed. Therefore hours of sitting at a desk without moving, head down, slumped can probably induce negative feelings too, wouldn't you agree?

Each state relies on a certain body positioning, to maintain it. This means that by changing the position of the body or the way we move, we can effectively change our 'state'!

****

Activity:

Take a moment now, to just jump up and down, dance to some music, stick your head out of the window, or sing a favourite song loudly.

As you do what you have chosen to do, pay close attention to the physical sensations that are happening.

Notice how your state changed. How did you feel?

****

Activity:

Improve your observation in recognising different states.

1. Ask a friend to remember a time when they felt in a very happy state. Notice as much

as you can about their expression, body posture and breathing and maybe how they sound if they are talking.

2. Ask a friend to remember a time when they felt in a 'down' state. Notice as much as you can about their expression, body posture and breathing, and how they sound, if they are talking.

3. Ask them to choose to remember another time when they are in either of those states (without telling you which one it is). Can you identify which state it is by seeing the physical changes?

Start noticing how your players look when they are feeling positive or negative, so that you help them to make changes to their state.

****

Our state is even affected by the way we dress. How do you feel and stand if you are wearing an expensive, elegant, suit? Even if you simply imagine dressing like that now, you can probably feel a difference in your state.

Have you noticed a difference in your players when they are turned out in full matching kit, as opposed to playing in jeans and T-shirt?

Eliciting states in others

As a coach, you are probably very aware of the importance of an athlete's state before competition, or even before a training session, because state has a dramatic impact on performance.

Have you tried to cheer your athletes up after they have lost, or underperformed; or tried to motivate them before an event? In any area of our lives, we have all affected someone else's state and often without meaning to!

You may be able to recall a time when you heard someone saying something like, "I don't know what got into him, I only said...................." In fact, every time we communicate we are eliciting states in other people. This is because they filter their experience of us through their filter system and come up with a meaning that affects their state!

The simplest way to purposely elicit a state in someone else is to ask them to remember a time when they felt that state in the past. To do this effectively, you should be in rapport with the person first and be 'doing' your version of that state too. For example if you want someone to be feeling happy and positive, you can think of a time when you felt that and get into the state first!

Use the script below to go deeper and create a strong state.

****

Activity

Work with a partner to practice the following

Ask your partner what state he/she would like to elicit.

Imagine being in that state first yourself to help lead your partner into that state.

Ask your partner to remember a time when he/she was in such a state, or ask them to make up a time when he/she was in such a state.

Being able to help your athlete elicit strong and powerful states and / or amplify weak ones is one of the most useful skills for a coach.

Question your partner

What can they see?

How big is the image? How far away? Moving or still? Colour or black and white? Bright or dim? Focused or unfocused? Associated or dissociated?

(associated means looking through your own eyes, dissociated means seeing yourself in the picture)

What can they hear?

Are they hearing from one point or all around? Loud or soft? Fast or slow? High or low pitch? Clear or muffled?

What can they feel?

Location in body? Breathing rate? Temperature? Weight? Intensity? Movement?

And you can also explore taste and smell

****

How to Change a Bad State

Sometimes you may find yourself or someone else stuck in a negative state. This could follow a 'break-up', a lost tournament or competition, a reaction to an argument, or a setback in some area of your life.

To change this state

Ask yourself how you might feel about it in five or even ten years time.

Imagine looking back from that time, and notice how unimportant it seems now. Perhaps from this viewpoint you can ask what you have learned from the old event. Is there anything about that old event that might now seem amusing to you?

Still in that future place imagine or see how things are going well for you, and access that feeling of positivity and well being. Walk into that future. Experience all those feelings fully, access all of your senses, and bring all that with you as you return back to the present.

Break States

States have a momentum all of their own, this means that just like a bike or a car in motion, we need to know the controls that make a change in direction.

Break state can be thought of as a way of interrupting the momentum and energy of any given or present state, changing it quickly.

Breaking the state is very important as it acts as a stepping stone or a bridging state from one to another. It is useful because some people find moving into a new state difficult, especially if they are far removed. For example, despondency/despair to excitement and motivation! A break state is therefore a neutral state.

A quick and easy way to break state in someone is to engage them in a 'transderivational search', this means that you ask them a random question, which is usually completely out of context in that particular situation, and for which the other person has to search for an answer!

Questions can be simple, such as; "What did you have for breakfast this morning?" "How did you get here?" "Have you ever considered the many colours that fruit can be?"

****

Activity:

Practice the following with friends who are not aware of what you are about to do:

1. Get into conversation with someone
2. Ask a random question and wait for their response
3. Continue the conversation like nothing happened

Note what happens, and think of times when you might find this skill useful to use

****

Activity:

Experiment with changing peoples' states.

1 When someone is in a 'miserable' or 'down' state, find a way to get them to move, and to raise their eyes upwards.

2 When someone is angry with you, get them to hold something in both hands. Take them by surprise as you ask them to hold whatever it is,

and make certain you keep a straight face as you do this.

****

Remember:

- An event is merely an event
- We are responsible or RESPONSE-ABLE for our states
- We are empowered to change our states when required or desired
- A state change can happen in seconds.

Action:

Think of how many ways there are to influence state. Consider music, lighting, videos, the way in which you speak and your body language.

How many ideas from this chapter do you already include, or could add into your coaching sessions, to create states of concentration, motivation, inspiration, excitement, enthusiasm and eagerness?

"Not he is great who can alter matter, but he who can alter my state of mind."

Ralph Waldo Emerson

"A good stance and posture reflect a proper state of mind."

Morihei Ueshiba

19

SIMPLE

ANCHORING

"Anchoring is the most effective technique I know for constructively channelling our powerful unconscious reactions so they're always at our disposal. It's a way to ensure that we always have access to our greatest resources."

Tony Robbins

Changing our 'state' instantly!

Have you sometimes heard athletes saying they were in the wrong frame of mind (state), when they lost a match or competition?

So often, people underachieve because they are not accessing all the resources available within themselves, either by not knowing they have these unexplored resources or lacking the knowledge in accessing the transferable resources from unrelated areas of their experience. They may lack the ability to create the right 'state'.

Anchoring is a process to create a positive or useful state immediately!

If you have an awareness of 'states' and can do visualisation then you will find Anchoring easy to use for yourself and to teach to your athletes.

You may already be aware that in the 1950's a Russian scientist; Ivan Pavlov conducted research on dogs whereby the dogs began to associate eating with a bell. Very quickly the dogs began to salivate whenever they heard a bell ringing. This experiment was named Classical Conditioning or Stimulus-Response and led to Anchoring. It is a process that enables you to access quickly and easily any state you require for any activity. For example, to execute a powerful tennis serve, or a perfect golf swing.

An anchor is any stimulus which generates a specific state inside you, and these are a part of our everyday life. For example, have you ever heard a certain piece of music that instantly transports you back to a specific memory? How many people respond rapidly to a certain glaring look in another's eye? Have you unexpectedly smelled a perfume that reminds you of someone, or a smell that reminds you of somewhere you have been a long time ago? Or even maybe just a simple certain touch by a lover that excites you immediately because you 'know what it means!' I am sure you recognise from the above list that anchors can be kinaesthetic, auditory, visual, and even olfactory (smell).

Methods of consciously setting your own anchor can be tactile such as squeezing your thumb and middle finger together or squeezing your earlobe. It could be auditory by saying a key word in a certain way. You might choose to create a visual anchor, maybe written words (affirmations?), a picture, or something you know will be present when you need it.

By practicing you will find that setting up an anchor is very simple to do and will effect a change of state when applied.

Anchors can be used at any time of your choosing. You may wish to be able to access confidence at any time and you can fire off your confidence anchor whenever you choose.

Creating and Setting a Resource Anchor

Preparation:

1. Select a resourceful state you would like to experience more often. For example self-confidence. When doing this, remember times, specific times in the past when you experienced this state strongly. You will need 3 to 5 different events. You can also choose a couple of resourceful states to use together that are of a similar energy. Make a list of those you can access easily, and

choose from that list; e.g. Enthusiasm, confidence, feeling strong, powerful, energised, might go together to create a confident state; another group of states could be calm, relaxed, peaceful, serene, and would create a relaxed state.

2. Select an anchor point. This is a part of your body that is not usually touched during normal everyday activities but is easily accessible to you. I would suggest an ear lobe, a knuckle or the skin between two fingers.

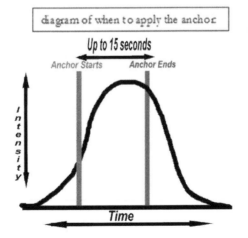

diagram of when to apply the anchor

Up to 15 seconds

Anchor Starts   Anchor Ends

Intensity

Time

Setting the Anchor

1. Close your eyes and recall a time, a specific time when you experienced the resource state; float down into your own body; see what you were seeing; hear what you were hearing; and really feel what you were feeling at that time, now.

2. Activate your chosen anchor (apply pressure to that point on your body) as soon as you feel the state strongly.

3. Release the pressure immediately the state begins to weaken. This is different for everyone and peak state with application of pressure could last up to 15 seconds. You won't need a watch - simply 'feel' it.

4. Open your eyes and break state, stand up and sit down again count to 10 or think of a cup of coffee, anything to ensure you have cleared your mind.

Repeat stages 1 to 4, three to five times using either the same resource state from different memories or a number of similar resource states as mentioned above. Every time you repeat it make each more compelling, notice more, feel more etc.

Of course you might want to set a couple of separate anchors to use different states in appropriate situations!

Test your anchor

Apply your anchor and notice that your associated resource state occurs spontaneously without any conscious effort. Apply the anchors again if necessary until you have easy access to your resource state.

Tips:

- Fire your anchors the same way every time you use them

- The anchor can be strengthened by repeating the process over several days

- If you find yourself in a real situation that creates the desired state, reset the anchor again to strengthen it

Remember:

- Anchors are used in every-day living

- We can trigger someone's anchor unknowingly or on purpose.

"We don't see things as they are, but rather as we are."

Anais Nin

20

GOAL SETTING

"I believe in goals. It's never a bad thing to have a dream, but I'm practical about it. I don't sit daydreaming about things that are impossible. I set goals and then work out how to achieve them. Anything I want to do in life I want to do well and not half heartedly."

Sir Richard Branson

What is a goal? In football it's a ball kicked into a net! It is also a target, something to reach for, to attain! To achieve anything, we must first identify what it is we want, and then we have to take as many actions as is needed to get there!

Goal setting is a major factor for motivating your athletes, and is linked to positive changes in self-believe, confidence and reducing anxiety. Goals represent a means of evaluating performance, and represent core values and beliefs about sport and success. Criteria that focus on self-improvement or effort are considered to be more positive than a focus on performance against others, though this is a simplified view because you need to take context into account. Are you developing an athlete from a beginner upwards, or is your athlete reaching the ultimate part of their career by competing in their last Olympic games where only a medal will do?

In the coaching environment do we actually know the specific goals, or ambitions, or even why each individual athlete is attending our sessions?

However, if you are coaching many large groups it is clear to see the challenges that face you in meeting the needs of each individual athlete, and in helping each one set their goals in an environment where there may be very many differences and abilities to deal with.

Athletes benefit from goal setting because their goals act as sign posts towards gaining their full potential or achievement in their chosen sport. Setting milestone goals aids motivation, charts progress and therefore increases self-esteem.

The coach benefits from setting goals with their athletes, because they can identify that their coaching is effective and make changes if necessary. When athletes meet their goals the coach can gain confidence, and prove they are effective as a coach. All of which reflects well on the coach's own personal performance and credibility.

I'm not going to suggest that you ask your athletes to fill in their goals or reasons for coming to you on a one to one basis, or that you organise your sessions into athletes who match in ability, or goals/desires, or that you set your own personal goal or coaching goal. Nor am I going to suggest how you record your goals and record all achievements. I am merely recommending the common SMARTER goal-setting technique and some other useful tools.

By understanding the concept of goal setting and actively using it, you will undoubtedly notice its full effectiveness for yourself.

Specific: What is it EXACTLY, that you want to achieve? For example "To run faster" would not be an effective goal. How fast specifically do you want to run, e.g. one mile in four minutes? For example: Poor goal: I want to play better clears. Good goal: I want to be able to hit 6 out of 10 clears from RC tramline to opposite RC tramline easily.

Measurable: How will you know when you achieve your goal? The goal must have a defined outcome e.g. I have got into the team. This is one way to measure your long term goal. How can you measure the stepping stone goals? Numerical goals are easy to measure and evaluate.

Action **Orientated**: What are you prepared to do to achieve this? Even more importantly what are you going to give up? This is an absolutely important part of goal setting. Everything comes at a cost!! If you are working with high performance athletes in any sport, will they have to give up other sports to focus on just one? Are they prepared to commit to possibly getting up early 5 or more times a week, more and heavier training sessions, and do they have the means to pay for more sessions/equipment/clothing etc? What will they possibly need to give up; time with friends, money to spend on other interests, alcohol, late nights?

Realistic: This is tricky because you don't want to be a 'dream-stealer', or put limits on your athletes, however, the goals set need to be realistic, so if you have an athlete who wanted to compete in the Olympics, and they were relatively new to your sport, you and they should consider: the athlete's health, fitness, age, time scale etc. Whilst goals need to be challenging, if the goal set is too difficult, the athlete will lose confidence, motivation and could leave the sport altogether.

Time framed: Set a date on the long-term or outcome goal and put earlier dates on the milestones, or stepping stone goals that need to be set in order to achieve the outcome.

Exciting and Evaluated: Is this goal and the stepping stone goals exciting enough to stay motivated. Evaluate your athlete's progress and celebrate their successes with them.

Recorded and Rewarded: Keep records. Write goals down and record results regularly. Rewarding success is a celebration of achievement, and it can be something to look forward to, especially when the going gets tough!

Why do we set goals?

- To maintain motivation by recording improvement

- To help to determine what is important, to give a direction, and to prioritise needs

- To help to improve performance by showing strengths and areas of development

- To help to stay focused

- To provide feedback on performance.

A goal may be a simple concept, but as the scale of the goal increases, so does its complexity.

A goal can be seen as the pinnacle of a pyramid. It only becomes real when everything else that had to occur before it is completed.

We usually think of milestones or small stepping stones, as methods of reaching any particular goal, and they are an easy way to identify what needs to happen in order to reach that goal.

However, as with even a simple goal such as baking an apple pie, some stepping stones may be done simultaneously, others have a definite sequence or order, while some can be carried out in any order as long as they get done.

For example, first there has to be a need or a desire/motivation to want an apple pie. Next, you would surely have to check where you are right now, by finding out whether you want a store bought pie or home-made pie, what money you have to spend, what ingredients you already have in the cupboard, or what you need to go and purchase. Also, what equipment is needed, or what you may need to buy or borrow. You might choose to cook the apples first, and allow them to cool, or would you rather make the pastry first and allow it to rest? When do you turn on the oven, before you begin the pie, or half-way through preparation?

Finally, the pie is completed and its quality depends on the ingredients and methods used in preparation! I am sure you may have been unfortunate enough to taste some pretty tough, sour, or sickly soggy pies haven't you? So the quality of the pie comes from what? The experience and knowledge of how to make light pastry, this includes the use of fingers, temperature of ingredients and hands during the mixing process, having the right amounts and ratio of ingredients, having the temperature just right, patience, commitment, effort, practice and so on. And of course, when the first pie doesn't work out as you like, you begin all over again, making changes, learning and gaining experience until eventually you have a pie from heaven. Perfect to your taste and palate, you have your ultimate goal! How long does it take you to get there? Well, we are all different aren't we? Some manage it the first time; others never get there and never bake another pie!

Oh, and of course, if you are one of those that managed to make your pie and eat it, you might want to set another goal, you might want more. Isn't that usually the case?

If that pie was a success, then how do we measure success? Think of any successes you have ever had. Would you agree that it is a feeling, an intangible element that is difficult to quantify? Try the feeling on for size right now, imagine something that has gone well, and then imagine something that went completely wrong! Are you aware that these are two completely opposite feelings? So, success is no less than an emotional state.

You have that emotional state inside you already. You can reference how to create emotional states in the anchoring chapter, but for now can we take it that achieving a goal = success = a 'good' feeling. By 'feeling' successful, we actually become more successful. Therefore, by excellent coaching we can inspire our athletes to 'feel successful' right from the start of their goal-setting, and seriously increase their chances of success!

Success is NOT something to wait for! We must have it NOW! It is a vital component in goal setting and it should run through every step of the way!

Goal Setting for You the Coach

How many coaches manage to set goals in their own coaching career? Whilst you can feel success at every point in your coaching career, do you aspire to be a great coach, or indeed, a master coach? If you do, you may personally define this in any number of ways. However, if you look at your goal to be an inspirational master coach, and to achieve coaching magic, what would you need to consider? Let's go through the apple pie pyramid again making it relevant to us as coaches.

What components make a good or a great coach?

****

Activity:

Using the triangle below, insert the characteristics that you feel are important to being a master coach.

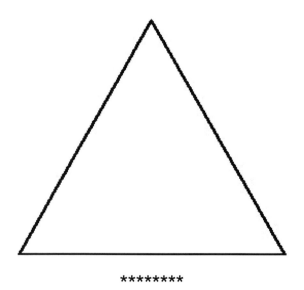

****

In the activity above, you may have come up with similar characteristics to the following:

Self-confidence, consistency, creativity, detail oriented, flexibility, friendliness, sense of humour/funny, good listener, independence, logical, motivational, objectivity, organised, outgoing, patience, resourcefulness, respectful, passion, sensitivity, empathy, effective speaking skills, well-roundedness, knowledge about the sport and people skills.

Whatever elements there may be in being a master coach, each coach will have their own personal strengths according to their personality types and life experiences. Gaining mastery is an on-going process, and a master coach can be working at grass roots with beginners and/or be working at the elite and performance end of sport!

Continual development x mentoring/coaching

=

Coaching Mastery

Performance Profiling

A performance profile will help you identify where you are right now, and the standard of performance you want to achieve. Doing this makes it easy to see your development areas.

Step 1

Identify the areas you think are important to you as a coach in your particular sport.

These are generally speaking broken into the following four key headings:

Communication skills

Listening, rapport, voice, language (positive/negative), body language, motivation and inspiration.

Organisational skills

Planning sessions, organising groups and practices, dealing with bookings, record keeping and other general admin duties.

In depth knowledge of the sport

This includes knowledge of tactics, technical, mental skills, physical needs and continuous professional development. Athletes will often be better performers of the sport than the coach. It is the coach's responsibility to ensure they have the coaching knowledge and skills to help each athlete achieve their own potential.

Motivation skills

This includes: goal setting, making practices fun and challenging, building self-esteem and confidence.

Step 2

Rate yourself on the qualities identified above. Rate where you are now and your target performance on a scale of 1-10 where 1 is a huge improvement required and 10 no improvement possible.

Step 3

Prioritise which areas you most need to work on, and quantify these from your ratings. For example where an overly quietly spoken coach measures himself 2/10 they may decide they want to improve to an 8/10.

See following tables as examples:

Factors do a performance profile on yourself as a coach. Rate yourself on a scale of 1-10 as suggested and fill in some specific details	?/10	Performance now - specific details	?/10	Target Performance - specific details
COMMUNICATION				
Listening Skills; athletes should feel that you are listening and valuing what they are saying without judgement or prejudice. Allow your athletes time to speak without jumping in and finishing their sentences. Accept what they say!				

Rapport; the ability to create close and harmonious relationships so that you can understand the other person and communicate well.			
Voice; projection, variety, tone timbre/ sound quality of voice, pitch, volume. It is a vital coaching tool for inspiring, motivating, keeping focus and interest and keeping authority.			
Language; you should be able to articulate, clear and concise with instructions. You should be focused on being positive (e.g. saying what you Do want not what you don't want). Words should be impeccable because your athletes should be able to trust you completely. Your language should teach, motivate and build confidence, self-esteem and self-belief.			
Body Language; your body language should be congruent with what you are saying. It should show strength, authority, and be used as a tool to convey enthusiasm, warmth, humour, and friendliness/			

General Communication; you are able to communicate effectively to other coaches, players and parents, and significant others. Additionally, you use newsletters, flyers, website, email, and other sources to convey your messages where relevant.				
Motivation and Inspiration; you use effective goal setting with our athletes which helps to motivate them and keep them on track. You understand how individuals differ in their motivation needs. You design practices that motivate; you inspire your athletes to be the best they can by being a positive role model and using excellent communication skills. You encourage your athletes to set, record and monitor their own goals, to create their own affirmations, and you celebrate their successes and help them recover and learn from their mistakes.				

ORGANISATION				
Planning sessions; you can plan sessions that show progressive, fun, challenging practices. The session planning takes into account the needs of the player so that you adapt your coaching style and planning to meet these needs. You are able to plan a whole series of sessions for one term/one year or more.				
Health and Safety; you are qualified for first aid, have a first aid kit to hand and have hazard check forms up to date. You have a register and player registration documents/details at every session. You keep all your players safe by checking the surroundings and ensuring you follow good practice guidelines.				

Organising of group; when you coach, your players can see and hear you easily, your practices give your athletes the best opportunity to practice effectively and safely. Your session has a structure that allows players to warm up, practice and cool down effectively. You give equal time, attention and personal feedback and value to every athlete.				
KNOWLEDGE				
Mental Skills; you know about the mental skills needed for the athletes' in their sport. You can observe and analyse their mental strengths and weaknesses, and are able to teach them techniques to control anxiety, fear, anger and to create positive states, positive thinking and positive self-talk. You can design practices to develop strong mental skills, good attitudes and build your athletes confidence levels continuously. You understand how your words affect the performance outcomes of your athletes, and are able to teach your athletes how to control their own inner voice.				

Technical; you can observe how an expert at the sport gets good results and can interpret, model and communicate this effectively to your own athletes by demonstration, verbal instructions, diagrams, videos, physical manipulation, etc. You produce effective practices for your athletes to model and develop these skills themselves, observing them, analysing and providing them with effective feedback which increases success in their own performance.			
Tactical; you have learnt by observation and instruction, and/or experience how the top athletes' get top results using good tactics. You are competent to observe, analyse your own athletes use of tactics compared to a top 'model' performer and can produce feedback and practices to help your athletes develop in this area.			

Physical; you have learnt by observation, instruction, and/or experience how the top athletes move in their chosen sport. You can observe and analyse all aspects of the required movement patterns, and can interpret and communicate the information to your own athletes, providing them with effective feedback, practices, and training programmes to teach and develop their own physical skills required for their sport.			
CPD (continuous professional development); you are committed to undergo continuous training in your coaching knowledge and have at least two courses per annum booked into your diary. You make a habit of reading and keeping up to date with new ideas. You have a personal coach, or a mentor to provide you with ongoing feedback and support. You network with other coaches and/or belong to a coaching group that supports and shares ideas. You keep your own coaching log or journal.			

Step 4

Develop a goal setting programme to help you achieve your goals. Select three goals that you would like to work on and identify where you are now (this is your starting point). Think of a strategy to meet them and the support required. Put a date on when you would like to achieve your goals, and make sure you can identify how you will know your goal has been reached.

Goal Planner (goals are best written in the present tense)	Specific Goals - Goal 1
Current Position (identify where I am right now)	
Strategy (What actions am I going to take)	
Support Required (Resources and people I need to help me)	
Time Scales (date to reach goal)	
Success Criteria (How I am able to identify and assess my progress)	

An example of a goal:

Goal Planner (goals are best written in the present tense)	Specific Goals - Goal 1
	I have set up and am running my own badminton (swap this for your chosen sport) club
Current Position (identify where I am right now)	*I am a league player with a love of the game, experience with working with groups of people and a passion to help them enjoy the game. I have no coaching qualifications or experience. I don't have much money, but do have time available.*
Strategy (What actions am I going to take)	*I need to gain knowledge and become qualified, gain experience, and research available venues. To do this I will take courses, and work alongside another coach*
Support Required (Resources and people I need to help me)	*Local sports development officers, badminton development officer, possibly my own club, a mentor coach, funding sources, local coaching steering group may help.*
Time Scales (date to reach goal)	*1 year - (insert a realistic date).*
Success Criteria (How I am able to identify and assess my progress)	*I have 20 young players playing in a four court hall, with me as their main coach. I feel excited, because my session is popular and the players are receiving excellent value and giving me great feedback. My sessions are cost effective: they are self supporting and give me an income of £25.00 per hour for on court coaching time.*

By clearly identifying exactly what you want to achieve, and where you are right now, you will be able to use your strategy to form some smaller stepping stones for your BIG goals.

For example, let's identify some actions that will need to take place in order to reach the above goal. For this we can do a mind map.

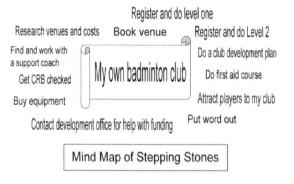

Register and do level one

Research venues and costs   Book venue   Register and do Level 2

Find and work with a support coach

Get CRB checked

Buy equipment

My own badminton club

Do a club development plan

Do first aid course

Attract players to my club

Contact development office for help with funding   Put word out

Mind Map of Stepping Stones

Once the main goal has been identified, it's time to put everything into action. It is important to record the achievement of your stepping stone goals because it keeps you focused. Measuring your achievements along the way allows you stay motivated on the journey, and I would suggest that each stepping stone achieved is celebrated, because the journey can also be enjoyed that way. When we feel successful it is a catalyst for even more success! Design a table such as the one above to record and monitor your own progress.

Performance Profiling With Your Athletes

Setting agreed goals that are relevant and accepted by your athletes means that they have control, ownership and ultimate responsibility for achieving their goals.

Profiling is a way to measure those characteristics or qualities of an athlete performing in his or her sport. The profiling process can be used for psychological, technical, and physical attributes such as movement, speed, balance, agility etc. The coach can identify the characteristics, or allow the athlete to list those they feel are important to them.

If you are instructing your athletes to identify the qualities, a good starting question to ask is:

"What do you think are the most important things/qualities that the top athletes have in common in our sport?"

You could show a video of some top performers, or put on a demonstration of top performers in action. If you don't have time in your coaching sessions, or if you prefer, you can simply identify the qualities of a top player in your sport yourself.

Write the qualities into a table or spread-sheet. The following example is specifically for badminton. Each player is to record how they perceive their own skills based on a scale of 1 to 10, where 1 is not at all or very poor and 10 is excellent. The bench mark could be based on their rating themselves against a national or top county player, shown in video or live performance.

By allowing an individual to make their own assessment of where they feel they are at the outset, and to monitor their own progress, they can be in control of their journey and their results. It takes courage to let go of the reins and give ownership to the player, but you as a coach can guide gently, using your questioning skills, video and other tools to create a sharp self awareness in your athletes.

MENTAL SKILLS	1	2	3	4	5	6	7	8	9	10
Confidence										
Concentration										
Emotional Control										
Commitment										
Enjoyment										
Fair play and good attitude to everyone										
Positive thinking and language patterns										
TECHNICAL	1	2	3	4	5	6	7	8	9	10
High singles serve										
Bh low and flick service										
Fh low and flick serve										
Fh/Bh net shots										
Fh/Bh net kills										
Fh/Bh net lifts										
Fh/Bh drives										
Fh/Bh smashes										
Fh clear										
Fh dropshot										
Fh smash										
Round the head hitting										
Bh clear										
Bh dropshot										
Glancing blows/slices										

MOVEMENT	1	2	3	4	5	6	7	8	9	10
Split step										
Lunge and recovery										
Transitions										
Weight Transfer										
Jumping & landing										
Fluidity (smoothness)										
Posture										
Balance										
Speed										
Power										
TACTICAL	1	2	3	4	5	6	7	8	9	10
Doubles										
Singles										
Mixed										

"What would you like to achieve by the end of this current school year?"

....

Once you and your athletes have agreed the current performance level, it is time to set goals. You might decide to stick to the criteria based on the characteristics of high level performance, or you could consider asking what the player would actually like to achieve within a certain time scale! A player might want to join a county squad, beat a friend or have any other personal goal.

Keep things simple by focusing on one goal from each section at most! See example below:

Stepping Stone Goal	Start Date	End Date	Method of Celebration
Level One Qualified Coach			
Find and work with a support coach			
CRB Check in place			
First Aid qualified			
Level 2 Qualified Coach			
Venues and costs researched			
Venue booked			
Club development planned			
Contact made with development officers			
Website created, posters			
Equipment purchased			

The goal setting tool above focuses only on four goals, one from each area of the sport.

The starting point notes are written in the past tense for a reason; talking about behaviours and actions we wish to change in the past tense, makes it easier to achieve success.

Each goal is as specific as possible and is written in the present tense, for the same reasons.

Outcome, Performance, or Process Goals?

Outcome goals: These focus on the end result, and in doing so, they can be harmful as they can often lead to de-motivation, because they depend upon so many uncontrollable factors. For example, you may achieve a goal to win a competition, but the opposition may be considerably weaker or injured.

This can leave you feeling de-motivated. On the other hand, even though you may have performed at your very best, and beaten your best time, the opposition still wins because they are even stronger than you. Choosing outcome goals requires considerable care.

Performance goals: These relate to the athlete's own performance and are safe because they are under the athlete's own control. For example, I want to lift 2lbs more weight in my next competition.

Process goals: These relate to the actions required to attain your goal. For example, a player with a poor lunge technique could focus on landing heel /toe. Process goals can consist of:

- Technical goals - such as length of stride

- Tactical goals - the race or game plan

- Physical goals - these are easier to set if you have scientific testing available but could include your diet or fluid intake

- Psychological goals -for instance, maintaining concentration for the whole race.

Making Goals More Powerful

Another way of looking at your goals is to list your current practices (e.g. physical or technical drills) and other habits (e.g. diet), and add 'so that....' to the end of each one.

For example: "I train with weights 3 times each week...so that...... I can increase my strength by 10% this season."

Adding 'So that' to your goal makes the goal more meaningful to the unconscious mind. This helps to add desire and to do what is necessary to achieve the goal.

If every 'so that' on your list can be followed by a goal or 'stepping stone', your everyday behaviours are in tune with your goals. If not, your behaviours could be unhelpful or unnecessary, or there may be other goals that you left unexplored.

The Lazy Coach Way!

If you want to encourage goal-setting and want a way of recording progress etc, but don't have the time, or are not into record keeping, you may wish to consider a simple yet effective means of doing so. Either issue every athlete with their own notebook or encourage them to get their own, to bring along to every session.

Athletes record their own goals and achievements from each session. You should write notes in these books based on your observations of each athlete, and use them to motivate, encourage, inspire, and give ongoing feedback. The books are very personal to each individual. My own athletes have been encouraged to cut out pictures of top performers, and paste their own face onto those bodies! This is excellent for visualisation! They should also record their personal affirmations.

The books are in action during the session and are close to hand for players to quickly record the measured goals set by the coach. The coach has access to them during, and at the end of the session, to note observations specific to individual athletes.

This is one of the goal setting methods I use with my athletes, and the players love their notebooks! Players write in their own books and invite other players and coaches to give written feedback into them. Players that use them fully, record the following:

- Match results; how they felt they performed and what they noticed about the opposition

- Training sessions; how they performed including record keeping of goals met during each session

- Coach's notes on the athlete's performance, and what requires more focus. Also praise for effort and attitude

- Pictures of top performers in action

- Personal goals

- Personal Affirmations and mantras

- Record of success and achievements (not necessarily for the sport!)

- Any homework such as flexibility exercises, visualisation work, etc.

My fellow coaches and I, carry our own notebooks to every session. We use them to record and reflect on our coaching performance and that of our players, and any thoughts on improving the sessions. A player writes feedback on the session on behalf of the group.

I treasure my notebook; it is full of testimonials from people who matter!

Action:

How are you going to incorporate goal-setting into your coaching sessions?

....

"When people say to me: "How do you do so many things?" I often answer them, without meaning to be cruel: "How do you do so little?" It seems to me that people have vast potential. Most people can do extraordinary things if they have the confidence or take the risks. Yet most people don't. They sit in front of the telly and treat life as if it goes on forever."

Philip Adams

"Obstacles are what you see when you take your eyes off your goals."

Anonymous

"What you get by achieving your goals is not as important as what you become by achieving your goals."

Zig Ziglar

21

GOAL SETTING

AND MOTIVATION

"A champion needs a motivation above and beyond winning."

Pat Riley

What is Motivation and why is it important?

Motivation causes us to act. We may eat because we are hungry, or we may enrol in an evening class because we want to gain knowledge.

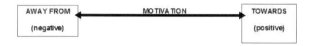

Motivation can be either positive or negative; neither of these forms is inherently good or bad! They both serve a purpose.

Negative motivation is an 'away from' motivator; when you do something because of fear, or want to avoid a certain outcome. For example, a child might revise every night for weeks on end because they don't want to fail an exam.

Positive motivation is a 'towards' motivator; when you do something because you have a great desire to reach a certain outcome and you enjoy the rewards of reaching that goal.

Intrinsic Motivation, generally, intrinsically motivated people act because their actions please themselves; they are in control of these themselves. They will have a desire to overcome the problem/task. They will have a feeling of pride and enjoyment in performing their skills.

Help these athletes by repeated goal setting, in order to progress and maintain their motivation.

Extrinsic, extrinsically motivated people act for reasons and rewards outside themselves and are therefore avoiding taking personal control.

These athletes enjoy tangible rewards such as medals and other prizes. Make sure you use this type of reward sparingly; otherwise you will create a situation where the winning of a prize becomes more important than the performance!

Intangible rewards such as praise and recognition of achievements, should be used on a regular basis to encourage your athletes to repeat positive behaviour patterns.

Remember:

- Goal setting is the biggest tool in motivating your players

- Allow your players to set their OWN goals! It is only your job to help them on their journey

- Some of your players won't want a goal, they will be happy to 'go with the flow' and the coach needs to respect this.

- Being motivated means that goals are achieved. How many different methods of motivating your own players can you think of to incorporate into your sessions now?

What actions are you going to take towards goal-setting with yourself and your athletes?

....

....

....

....

....

....

....

*"Ability is what you're capable of doing.
Motivation determines what you do. Attitude
determines how well you do it."*

Raymond Chandler

MOVING FORWARD

"You are always a student, never a master. You have to keep moving forward."

Conrad Hall

You have taken big steps towards being a truly exceptional and highly regarded coach. However, reading and knowledge is nothing without application, therefore go out and practice your skills. Eventually, with repeated use, you will have integrated them into your communication system which means you will be using language patterns without even thinking about it and getting some great results.

When you practice the ideas here for yourself, you will discover that your own future is unobstructed, that you are present to the opportunities to influence that are abundant in the world of coaching, and that you are able to affect a person for the rest of their life!

Coach with **PASSION**

INSPIRE your players

CREATE Winners in life!

"You cannot open a book without learning something."

Confucius

"Change is the end result of all true learning."

Leo Buscaglia

ABOUT SUE RUTSON

I have had a fabulous time coaching my favourite sport for over 24 years. At the start, I had many doubts about whether I could be good enough and whether I knew enough, after all, I hadn't played nationally - not even for my county! I was merely an enthusiastic - admittedly VERY enthusiastic club player. I remember driving home in tears from my first training days because I felt useless! I had to learn to coach techniques I hadn't even mastered myself!

From such a humbling start I braved it into coaching and started with beginners. Surprisingly - so it seemed to me back then, within the first two years, my players were beginning to win league matches and were being invited to county cells!........................ Hmmmm, maybe I could coach after all!

Coaching has continued onwards and upwards and has been both a great joy and absolute satisfaction. I have learned from my own experience and from many years of observing coaches, that there is a vital edge to coaching...........a magical ingredient! You don't necessarily have to have been at the top of the game to help someone else get to the top! Athletes need many coaches during their training years to get to the top. Master Coaches are needed at every stage of the journey. I am very fortunate indeed to have found the magic and to use it to get fast results for my athletes who want to perform to their highest potential. I am grateful for the privilege of working with wonderful athletes and privileged to share the magic with coaches who also want to be the best they can be; whatever sport they coach.

For information on practical courses on all the ideas in this book plus far more, contact:

sue@inspiration-coaching.com

Printed in Great Britain
by Amazon